ENDORSEMENTS

Willie Jolley has written another incredible self-empowerment guide that will enable you to "snatch victory from the jaws of defeat." This powerful, timely survival manual will expand your vision and teach you how to succeed where others are failing. It will help you to develop the mindset and skill set to convert setbacks into cash.

—LES BROWN
best-selling author, award-winning speaker,
and television and radio personality

This book is full of change and challenge, pride and power, significance and success. Willie Jolley is an emotional power source whose energy is just barely contained in this wonderful book. When you open it, you'll feel the vitality of unrealized choices, and when you close it, you'll feel energized to change your life for your own benefit and for those around you.

—ALAN WEISS, PhD
author of *Million Dollar Consulting* and *Thrive!*

In this book, Willie Jolley hits a home run on the topic of personal and professional success and wealth building! Read it and then re-read it...and then tell everyone you know to get a copy and read it! That way everyone you know will grow their wealth!

—LARRY WINGET
television personality and best-selling author of
You're Broke Because You Want to Be and
Your Kids Are Your Own Fault

Willie Jolley is committed to developing wealth in people around the world, and this book is a true example of that commitment! Read it, and you will be inspired and empowered to grow your success and your wealth!

—KELVIN BOSTON
host of the *Moneywise* series on PBS-TV,
and author of *Who's Afraid to Be a Millionaire?*

Willie Jolley has written a book, *Turn Setbacks into Greenbacks,* that will empower and inspire you to greater success and achievement! I highly recommend reading this book!

—WALLY AMOS
best-selling author, speaker, positive thinker,
and founder of The Cookie Kahuna cookie company

I know Willie personally, and if you are with him for even a minute, he will get you charged up about something in your life. He can't help it. Motivation just pours out of him. He is a man on a mission to get all of us to see that our dreams might have been deferred but they don't have to die. His advice doesn't come with budget sheets or investment tips but inspiration to persist and persevere in tough economic times.

—MICHELLE SINGLETARY
Nationally Syndicated Personal Finance Columnist,
The Washington Post
author of *The 21 Day Financial Fast:
Your Path to Financial Peace and Freedom*

To Jahmiel

Keep the faith!
and Fly High!
God Bless You

turn

SETBACKS *into*
GREENBACKS

turn
SETBACKS *into*
GREENBACKS

7

STEPS *to go from*
financial DISASTER
to financial FREEDOM

DR. WILLIE JOLLEY

Publisher's Note: this book was first published in 2010. Not all references to economy and conditions have been updated. We think you'll agree that the messages contained in this book are timeless.

Disclaimer:

While efforts have been made to verify information contained in this publication, neither the author nor the publisher assumes any responsibility for errors, inaccuracies or omissions.

While this publication is chock-full of useful, practical information; it is not intended to be legal or accounting advice. All readers are advised to seek competent lawyers and accountants to follow laws and regulations that may apply to specific situations.

The reader of this publication assumes responsibility for the use of the information. The author and publisher assume no responsibility or liability whatsoever on the behalf of the reader of this publication.

SOUND WISDOM

P.O. Box 310

Shippensburg, PA 17257-0310

This is an updated, revised edition of *How to Turn Setbacks into Greenbacks*.

For more information on foreign distribution, call 717-530-2122.

Reach us on the Internet: www.soundwisdom.com.

Cover Design: Eileen Rockwell

ISBN: 978-0-7684-0888-1

ISBN Ebook: 978-0-7684-0889-8

For Worldwide Distribution, Printed in the U.S.A.

1 2 3 4 5 6 7 / 19 18 17 16 15

DEDICATION

I dedicate this book to my children, LaToya and William. And to my brother's children, Victor, Vincent, Rashida, Vivian, Christina, Noble Jr., and Nathan, who became my children when their father (my brother) passed away. I have done my best to teach each of you wealth-building principles. I pray you use them and make a point to share them with generations to come!

I also dedicate this book to my family members who have made their transition since my last book. To my mother, Catherine B. Jolley; my brother, Noble Jolley Sr.; my father-in-law, Reverend Rivers S. Taylor Sr.; and Aunt Eunice Ragland...I say this privately and publicly, "I could curse because you are gone, but I choose to celebrate that you came this way! I will always love you!"

ACKNOWLEDGMENTS

I want to thank my wife, Dee Taylor-Jolley, for her continuous support and inspiration. I want to thank my children, William and LaToya, for their input in this project. I want to thank my marketing manager, Cheryl Ragin, for her help in getting this book finalized and ready for print.

I want to thank the members of my Mastermind Group, Bill Cates, Steven Gaffney, Zemira Jones, and Suzi Pomerantz, for their advice and input as I started throwing around the concept of the book. I want to thank my dear friend Sam Horn (www.samhorn.com); she is a genius when it comes to putting literary ideas into a catchy concept. As I started to work on this concept of helping people create wealth even in the midst of a recession, I struggled with how to put it in a succinct title. I was considering a few titles, including "How to Turn Economic Setbacks into Comebacks," "How to Go Up in Down Economic Times," "How to Get through the Recession and Get Rich," and a few others about making money in tough economic times.

During that time, I attended a networking dinner Sam hosted for some of her friends, and I mentioned my ideas. She said, "Willie, your book *A Setback Is a Setup for a Comeback* has created a new catchphrase that many people around the world have made a common part of their vernacular. You are now well-known as the Comeback Guru, because of the book and your PBS special, *Turning Setbacks into Comebacks*—but now it sounds like you want to talk about creating a financial comeback, and so you are talking about focusing on the greenbacks!" I said, "Sam, you are absolutely right!" I want to thank Sam Horn for her genius and her willingness to share it.

CONTENTS

THE FORD MOTORS SETBACKS TO GREENBACKS EXPERIENCE!

Have you or someone in your family ever had a Ford Motor car at some time in the history of your family? If you are like most people I ask, your response was "Yes!"

For many years, Ford Motors was the leading car manufacturer in the United States, with over 50% market share. Yet over time, Ford lost that position, and in 2005 hit bottom. Their share market had fallen from 50% to around 15%. They went from being profitable to losing millions every month and being on the brink of bankruptcy.

For the first time ever, Ford brought in a new CEO from Boeing. His name was Alan Mulally, and he had developed a reputation for transforming and turning around organizations. Mulally had been successful in turning Boeing around.

When Mulally joined Ford, his first goal was to get the right people on his team. He wanted to then reduce the bloated work force. There was a need to get Ford employees, who had worked for company for 30 to 40 years to either retire or move on to do something else. Plus, he needed to get his team to have a mindset focused on excellence. He immediately needed 25,000 people to leave... but did not want a layoff. That would have been a public relations nightmare.

Instead, Mulally decided to offer the workers an amazing buyout to leave voluntarily. They were offered $100,000 cash, plus four years health insurance and four years college tuition to learn a new trade. The offer was put in place in early 2006, but by September of that year, only about 4,000 people had taken the offer.

You might wonder why people would not take advantage of such a generous opportunity. Well, imagine you worked for Ford, and your father worked for Ford, and your grandfather before him worked for Ford. All you knew was Ford. Your whole world perspective centered around Ford. In addition, imagine that in good times, when there were three shifts in the plants and an abundance of overtime, you could easily make six figures. If you brought in six figures and your spouse also worked for Ford, then you had a significant household income. You might have a house in Detroit, plus a vacation home in the Upper Peninsula of Michigan and an RV to transport you from one place to another.

As Ford struggled financially and asked these people to take the buyout, many declined for they were waiting for the good times to return! Yet, like in the classic book, *Who Moved My Cheese*, the cheese had moved.

In September of 2006, the Ford Executive team called me and said one of their executives had read my book, *A Setback Is A Setup For A Comeback*. Their research showed I had a reputation for positively influencing the behaviors of others!

Ford wanted me to motivate and influence their people to leave and take their buyout! I laughed and said I could not motivate people to leave their jobs. But, if they would allow me to, I would share my story of how I was a broke and busted nightclub singer, who got fired and replaced by a karaoke machine, yet decided to change my thinking and change my life! If I could share what I learned in the midst of my mess, I felt I could have the same impact on their thinking—to get them to dream bigger!

The Ford team agreed that I should tell my story and the results were amazing. Ford's goal was to get 25,000 people to take the buyout. When the final tallies came in, over 38,000 had taken the buyout!

That was 2006. In 2007, Ford asked me to come to Detroit to record video messages they could play every day in the lunch rooms about excellence and the power of a positive attitude. Then in 2008, Ford asked me to do another tour to talk to the employees about going the extra mile and the impact they could have on the company's comeback.

In 2009, Ford was the only one of the big three U.S. auto makers to be able to reject a government bailout. America loved their being able to survive without the government's help. Within months of Ford rejecting the bailout, they went from losing a million dollars a month to making a billion dollars a month. They turned their setbacks into real greenbacks! And you can too!

This book will give you some principles that you can use to turn your setbacks into incredible comebacks, and even into greenbacks!

Read it.

Act on it.

Then share your amazing comeback to greenback stories with me and the entire world!

Send me an email at info@williejolley.com and put in the title, My Setbacks to Greenbacks story. We look to hear the great comeback stories!

FOREWORD

"I don't believe in a law to prevent a man from getting rich; it would do more harm than good. So while we do not propose any war on capital, we do wish to allow the humblest man an equal chance to get rich with everybody else."
—ABRAHAM LINCOLN

Lincoln understood what many do not. In a creative, free enterprise society like the United States, many aspiring and motivated citizens can still work hard to save, then to invest, and ultimately to become entrepreneurs or owners of capital to create their own wealth.

The American Dream is alive and well. You have every right, even a responsibility, to live your dream. Those who say that we're in a time when there are no opportunities just don't know where to look.

Help is on the way, and you are holding it right now. Willie Jolley's timely and informative book, *Turn Setbacks into*

Greenbacks, appeals to your best hopes, not your worst fears, to your confidence, rather than your doubts. Finally, a book that puts the focus where it belongs—what you can do now to ensure your own economic future by putting the insights and strategies provided into action.

Sounds too good to be true! In this age of constant change and continuing economic uncertainty, waiting for someone else to hand you the lifestyle and success you want is just wishful thinking. Forget waiting for the Tooth Fairy, the Fairy Godmother, or government politicians! Get rid of any thought of victim thinking—the obstacles you face and the answers you seek don't come from others. You have what it takes to be a resilient and optimistic achiever.

Optimism isn't developed through repeating positive thinking mantras about how great life is, in the absence of evidence. This isn't motivational hype. Research shows that optimism is earned through a track record of overcoming obstacles. The more obstacles you overcome, the more you believe that you can overcome the next one. Optimists are realists. They want to know the problems they face, because they believe they can overcome or get around them to become successful. This book won't give you wealth; you'll have to earn it one day, one choice, one action at a time.

This information-rich book provides a proven roadmap. You will learn the financial skills, the plan and attitudes you need to achieve your own American Dream. You'll learn how to keep hope alive in this age of cynicism by trading feelings of helplessness and frustration for resilience, resourcefulness, and persistence as you turn adversity and obstacles into financial opportunities.

The only person you even remotely control is yourself; so get busy investing your worry time in a constructive action plan one day at a time. Every successful entrepreneur will tell you that the journey to wealth is filled with closed doors, setbacks, failures, and the satisfying joy of achieving success along the way. Don't let anyone make you a victim; you are a resilient achiever who is choosing to live your dream. Wealth should not be your primary goal; it is the by-product of transforming your gifts and innovative ideas into a mission that makes a difference people are willing to pay for. When you find your gifts, identify your mission, focus your efforts, and claim a positive attitude, wealth and meaning are around the corner!

As a speaker and inspiring motivator, I've seen Willie Jolley in action. His advice and common sense insights are as enlivening as they are empowering. He's been where you've been, and he's taken his own journey to success after success. Now, he's ready to give you the lessons learned along the way.

Willie Jolley not only informs and energizes, he communicates in ways that people can understand and appreciate. His book highlights some *keepers* that I can't wait to use:

- The bad times have come and will pass; they came to pass...not stay!

- Leave victim thinking to others—if 10% are unemployed, 90% are working. Be one of the victors, not one of the victims.

- Don't do what's comfortable—do what's necessary.

- Be proactive—get up and get going!

- Success won't come to you—sell and market by talking to people about your business, your products, and your services.

- When you pray, move your feet so God has something to work with!

All it takes for your dreams to become true is for you to claim it for yourself. Do something better that costs less. Do it better or faster. Innovate and make a move. If early attempts fail, get up and make new choices...and succeed. How do you start? If you are not sure what to do first, start by getting up and doing something really simple...read this book! By the way, when you finally do succeed, be ready to write Willie about what worked for you in making your dream live. He just may use your story on a motivational minute message. You may even read about yourself in his next book.

So, devour Willie Jolley's *Turn Setbacks into Greenbacks* and get busy turning your worries into profitable opportunities one day at a time. Don't just read it once; reread the parts that fit you and share the insights learned with others. Finally, give the author the greatest compliment by putting the insights into action to help turn your life around! Remember, delivering on your economic dreams is both your opportunity and your responsibility.

TERRY PAULSON, PhD
Professional speaker, national columnist, and author of
*The Optimism Advantage: 50 Simple Truths to
Transform Your Attitudes and Actions into Results*

PREFACE

"Money, money, money, money...money!" Those are the lyrics from the hit song "For the Love of Money," by the O'Jays. The song was a massive hit for them in the 1970s, and it is still popular today. In fact it was the song chosen as the opening theme for the popular show *The Apprentice,* with Donald Trump, in which contestants compete to work for Donald in the hopes of making a lot of, you guessed it, money. Let's face it, money is a popular topic in popular music and in mass media, with shows like *Fast Money, Mad Money, Who Wants to be a Millionaire*, and *Who Wants to Marry a Millionaire?* There are entire magazines and newspapers dedicated to money—making it, saving it, investing it—you name it. Money is a major part of our global culture.

Yet we have all heard the saying, "Money isn't everything!" To that I want to say I agree, money is not everything, *but...* money certainly is an important thing—a VERY important thing! When times get tough, money's role as a necessary part of our lives becomes even clearer. Money is important, and so we must talk about it and develop skills to generate money and manage the money we generate.

IS IT REALLY NECESSARY TO TALK ABOUT MONEY?

Occasionally over the years I have one person or another come up to me after a speech and ask why I must talk about money. They say life is about more than money. My answer to this is always the same: I could not agree more! Life is about so much more than money.

I have said it in earlier books, and I will say it again now: Money is a powerful motivational tool, it is a powerful motivator! Money will motivate people to get up earlier, and stay up later. Money will motivate people to go where they don't want to go, and do things that they don't want to do. Money will make people go to jobs that they hate and will motivate them to keep going over and over again. YET, money is not the most powerful motivator! I believe that money is a powerful motivator, but love is much more powerful. I ask you to stop and go with me through this following scenario.

Assume someone came up to you and offered you $1,000 to walk on a board that is 100 feet long and 2 feet wide. The board is laid on the ground, and all you have to do is walk down the board from one end to the other. Would you walk the board for $1,000? I hope you say "Yes" because that would be an easy $1,000. Now let's say that the same person took that same board to the top floor of a 100 story skyscraper. (I might have to put a brick on the $1,000 bill to keep it from blowing away with the winds at the high altitude.) Would you still walk the board from end to end while 100 stories above the ground, for $1,000? Most people I ask say, "No!"

Now stop and think a moment about someone you love, maybe a parent, or your child, or your brother or sister or best friend. Now imagine that the person who wanted you to walk on the board was holding your loved one on the hundredth floor at the other end of the board between the skyscrapers, and the person told you that if you didn't walk the board, your loved one would be thrown off the building. Would you be willing to walk the board now? Most people I have asked say, "Yes! Without question or doubt, yes!" When all is said and done, people will do more for love than they will do for money. Money is important but it is not everything.

Life is about family and friends and the faith; but when we are short of money, it becomes a pressing concern on our minds. For most people, money is important but does not really take all of our focus. But when we get to a place where we don't have any money, then it becomes a big thing and the predominant issue that preoccupies our thinking.

I have noticed that the people who usually say that money is not important are the ones who have money or at least know where their next meal is coming from and have no fear of losing their home. But if you don't have money for food and you have fears about where you will sleep, money tends to be a greater issue. The only people who truly do not care about money are those who have taken a vow of poverty or whose theology states that there is piety in poverty. However, I only get this response from one or two people every now and then. The other 98 percent of the people I talk to after my speeches are either looking for ways to increase their income so they either help their families live better lives or are looking for ideas to create more revenue so they can give more money.

I want to say right up front that in this book I will talk about money, and how you can get more money, even in tough economic times. I want to talk about the fact that money is an important and necessary part of our society. Some people feel that money is not important and not good to talk about in public conversation. Others feel that money is bad and is the "root of all evil," yet the Scripture actually states that "the *love* of money is the root of all evil." It is when money becomes your god that it becomes a terrible master. Having money is usually not the problem, but it is a problem when money has you!

If the love of money is the root of all evil, then lack of money is what causes the evil tree to sprout and grow. In tough economic times, we can actually see how money—and the lack of it—can cause people great amounts of anxiety and grief and can make them do terrible things. When money becomes tight, it touches every part of your life and lifestyle. Plus when it becomes tight for a community, it impacts every part of the community and culture, from the amount of money people spend for their recreation to the amount of money people donate to their church. No one is immune to the sting of the economic pinch. When people have no money, or are afraid to spend the money they have, it can bring economies and countries to their knees.

During the tough times, the tails fall out, revealing the wolves who are hidden in sheep's clothing during the good times. Bernie Madoff is a perfect example of a wolf in sheep's clothing. He "made off" with the life savings of thousands of hardworking people who had invested everything they had with him. As we all know now, he was running the biggest Ponzi scheme in history.

During tough times, people become frightened and stop spending money. When people stop spending money on items like homes and cars, that has an impact on the workers who make and sell homes and cars, and those people have less money to spend on the regular items of necessity. And the cycle continues so that it eventually affects everyone.

The lack of money can have an overwhelming impact on a society. Money is not everything, but it is very important to life. As Rita Davenport says, "Money is not everything... but it is right up there with breathing!"

Sometimes the tough economic times have nothing to do with the world's economy but have to do with your personal economy. In other words, there might be times when the economy is healthy, but you have hit a bump in the road and you are in need of a personal economic recovery. Either way, whether you have lots of money or you are experiencing a lack of money, these situations can play a major part in your stress levels and in your health and wellness.

WHY IS IT IMPORTANT TO BE WEALTHY?

"Money can't buy happiness, but neither can poverty." —LEO ROSTEN

I ask why it is important to develop personal wealth because, deep down, most people ask themselves how they can make more money, but only a few know why, and even less go beyond the question to take action to make wealth a reality. If I asked the question, "Who wants to be a millionaire?" most people would say, "I do!" The people who answered in the positive really would like to become millionaires, but very few actually make it happen, because to them wealth is about luxurious living and extravagance, not about practical day-to-day existence. In contrast, I say that wealth is not about extravagance and living in the lap of luxury but rather about living the kind of life that offers you and your loved ones the best opportunities for health and longevity.

Most people want to be wealthy, but very few have decided that it is *important* to be wealthy. I say that it is important to be wealthy! Why? Because money gives you options. Money gives you options for many important aspects of life including housing, health care, and education.

As I travel around the world giving speeches, I often meet people who say they want more money, yet have not made the decision to take the necessary actions to create additional income. These people do not understand that money creates longevity, because the lack of money has a negative impact on your peace of mind and your stress level. Statistics show that poor people tend to have shorter life spans because of the lack of preventive health programs, exercise programs, and adequate health care.

Some years ago, I heard a story about a young boy who developed a strange growth on his leg. His mom took him to her health care provider, where the doctor examined the young boy and said that he had a rare illness. His recommendation was to amputate the boy's leg at the knee.

The mother was stunned and told the doctor that the young boy was a very talented soccer player, and she wondered what other options were available. When the doctor replied that amputation was the most efficient way of handling the illness, the mother asked if she could get a second opinion, and she was directed down the hall to another doctor.

The second doctor looked at the chart and came to the same conclusion, that amputation at the knee was the most efficient way of handling the situation. The mother again proclaimed that the young boy was a gifted athlete and loved running and playing sports, and she hoped that maybe there were other options besides amputation. The doctor shrugged and said, "Sorry, but that is the most efficient way to handle the situation."

The mother then began to research and found that the illness was not life threatening, although it was serious, and that amputation was not the only option. She approached the health care provider again to get another opinion on the matter, but was told that her plan only allowed two opinions on the same item. She told the lady on the phone, "I appreciate your candor, but I have a little money in the bank, so I will check out some other options on my own."

The mother searched the Internet and found a specialist in Baltimore, Maryland. She contacted his office and set up an appointment. He was not a participant in her health care plan, so she had to pay for the visit out of her own pocket. She reminded herself, "I have some money so I will pay for the visit." She and her son flew to Baltimore and the specialist spent a considerable amount of time with the young boy. Finally he finished the exam and said, "I am sure you were told that amputation was the best way to handle this problem, but I don't agree. It is the most efficient and cost-effective way to handle the problem, but it is not the only way or the best way to handle the problem." He continued, "I can save your son's leg. It will not be cheap, but I can save his leg." The doctor went on to perform the treatment, and save the young boy's leg. This is just one example that, yes, although money is not *everything,* it does give you options.

This raises a rather interesting question: How do we handle the anxieties that appear when we realize that we have a lack of money? The answer is further in this book...along with not only surviving tough economic conditions, but thriving. That's right, *thriving!* I will take you on a journey that demonstrates how to handle economic downturns, both financially and mentally, and shows what it will take for you to face your financial fears and win in spite of the economic situation you are facing. It will help you get a winner's attitude about wealth.

I mentioned dealing with money and our attitude to money because our attitude has a big impact on how we handle money, especially in tough times. It doesn't even take a full-on depression for people to get depressed and overwhelmed by the gloom and doom of tough economic times. However, we can turn an economic setback into an advantage and position ourselves for super success and wealth. This is the time for *you* to become wealthy!

Depressions, recessions, economic downturns, or simply being broke and having more month than you have money, it all leads back to the same place: WE NEED MONEY! Money is important, and most people not only need money, they need a lot more money—especially if they have children. Then you need LOTS OF MONEY!

There was a time in my life when I would have said, "Money is not important, it's the love of friends and family that is really important!" I have learned over the years that I was half right. Ultimately, the love of friends and family is the most important. We all know that when we come to our last days, we will not think about the money we have but the love of friends and family. But without money, that last day may come much earlier than it could. Having money does not guarantee long life, but statistics clearly show that people with means tend to live longer than those without money.

In my earlier books, I talked about the importance of friends and family and how you must nurture those relationships, because when all is said and done, they will be the most important parts of your life. I still believe that is true, but money must be on your list of important items or you will stress the seams of the relationships. When tough times hit and you have children to feed and bills to pay, you come to the realization that money is very important. I have found the tighter the economy gets, the more money becomes a focus, so let's deal with it, learn how to get through the tough times, and get on the road to wealth.

As mentioned earlier, the subject of money permeates our culture; we cannot escape it. Money is everywhere. It is in our literature and in our magazines. There is even a magazine called *Money Magazine.* There are many newspapers, such as *The Wall Street Journal,* that focus on money and financial news. And even my favorite book, the best-selling book of all time, the Bible, speaks about money more than 2,300 times. In Ecclesiastes 10:19, the translation by Peterson reads, "Laughter and bread go together, and wine gives sparkle to life. But it is money that makes the world go round!" According to Howard Dayton, former chief executive officer of Crown Financial Ministries, 15 percent of everything Jesus says is about money.

And in Deuteronomy 8:18 the Bible says, "And you shall remember the Lord your God, for it is He who gives you power to get wealth, that He may establish His covenant which He swore to your fathers, as it is this day!" That means that God gives us the power and ability to get wealth, yet the wealth must be to establish His covenant, which is to help others. I believe that God wants His children to be wealthy, and He will help you to become wealthy if you are willing to be a good steward of that wealth and show a pattern of using your wealth wisely.

My goal is to help you to create wealth and have money. I want to help you create not just financial wealth, but also success in your personal and family relationships. I want to help you to turn your economic setbacks into exciting comebacks—in fact, to turn your setbacks into greenbacks!

A LITTLE BACKGROUND

Before we get into the meat of this book, I think it is important for me to share a little about myself. I am an inspirational/motivational speaker, singer, radio and television host, and author, and I have been blessed to write books and create programs that have become best-sellers around the world. For the past quarter century, I have made it my business to learn as much as I can about success and to share that knowledge with millions of people via speeches, books, radio, television, columns, music, Internet, email, and other forums—even a daily Willie Jolley Wake-Up Call. I have had the opportunity to develop friendships with numerous millionaires and billionaires, and have learned incredible lessons from them about life and success. I also want you to know that as much as this book is about finances and getting rich, that information is secondary. The primary insight that I will share in this book is how you will personally grow, and how this growth will manifest itself into financial success and stability.

I want to state emphatically that I am grateful that I can live in a time when I can talk about my faith, my family, and my thoughts about money openly. I can state emphatically that I am pro-God, pro-family, and pro-free enterprise! I thank God for life and for the great blessings He has given me. Of all the things I am grateful for, the most important thing to me, beside my faith, is my family. As we juggle our many responsibilities in life, we must make sure to take extra special care of the family ball, because that is the one made of glass, while the others are made of rubber. If you drop the other balls, they will bounce, but if you drop the family ball it may very well shatter, and many times, it cannot be put back together again. So I recommend you take special care of the family ball, because it is precious and very fragile.

Finally, I am in favor of free enterprise. I believe we live in a time and a place where all things truly are possible, and that the level of your thinking ultimately determines the level of your impact and your income! So I recommend you dream big, think big, do big, and reap the benefits in a big way!

Now that you know where I stand, you can understand what I will say and why I will say what I say, and you can take the information that follows and craft a greater existence and a better life!

So let's get it on! Let's *go big!*

Let's turn setbacks into greenbacks!

PROLOGUE

In the midst of the global recession of 2008, one day I was watching television and heard a news story about a young man who had lost his job, had run out of money, and lost all, and the unfortunate decision to end his life. He made a permanent decision as the result of a temporary problem. He took his life over a temporary problem and that was a decision that could not be reversed. I screamed and hollered at the television "No! There are other options!"

Over the next few days after that news report, I heard other stories about people making drastic decisions about their futures, as a result of a lack of money. I realized that I needed to do something and do it immediately to help people see their economic setbacks from a different perspective, a positive perspective! I knew I needed to give people some hope, even in the midst of what might have been a hopeless time for them. And I knew that I had some information that could not only help them find hope, but also help them find solutions to their financial despair.

I quickly contacted some friends in the publishing industry and asked them if they would be willing to change their release schedules to add one more book. I was pleasantly surprised that I immediately got a "Yes," and I went to work on quickly finishing the manuscript and getting it to them in record time. Within six months of that conversation, the book was out, in bookstores and flying off the shelves. It quickly hit a number of best-sellers lists.

After the recession had receded and the economy was getting back to normal, I realized that my level of letters and emails about financial situations had not receded. People were still emailing me asking for help in getting their finances in order. People were still having money issues and economic setbacks and needed help. I learned that even though the global economy had improved, does not mean that the economies of individuals will improve. So I decided to create an updated, revised version of the book to help people who are struggling with their economic setbacks, no matter how they found themselves in that setback situation.

This is the revised version of the book that is designed to help you turn your economic setbacks into great economic comebacks! In fact this is the book especially designed to help you turn those economic setbacks into greenbacks!

MONEY MATTERS

If you have had financial challenges—lost your job, your home, or your savings—and if this makes you think that you are about to lose your mind, then this book can help! And if you have not had any challenges with money, I definitely recommend you read this book, because if you live long enough, you will eventually have some economic setbacks.

I want to say that this book is about money! Money plays a major part in our daily activities—from what we eat, to where we sleep, and the level of comfort we have in our lives. Money is important. Some people say that money makes the world go round, and I would not disagree that money does make things happen all around the world, and that money does matter! And since money matters, we might as well talk about it and help people develop a healthy perspective on money and how to increase their prosperity, even in tough economic times. We need to talk about wealth and why it is important to not only turn our setbacks into comebacks, but also turn our setbacks into greenbacks! (Greenbacks is a slang term for the green paper money we use in the United States.)

Introduction

THE SECRETS TO TURNING SETBACKS INTO COMEBACKS

We will all have setbacks in life—not maybe, not might, but for sure. We will all have setbacks in life. Before we talk about how to turn setbacks into greenbacks, I think we need to review the basics of turning setbacks into comebacks. In my book *A Setback is a Setup for a Comeback,* I interviewed people who had incredible setbacks and were able to turn them into amazing comebacks. Some of the people I wrote about were famous, like Lee Iacocca, Wally Famous Amos, and Les Brown. But they were famous...what about the people who might not be famous or might not have a lot of money? Would these principles work for them as well? The answer is a resounding "Yes!" In fact, the stories that inspired me the most were the stories of everyday people who had setbacks and turned them into great comebacks.

Like the young man I interviewed who had a small business and two small children, and was struggling to provide for his family. He had a setback with his business and went bankrupt. He lost his house and ended up living on the street, but that was not the end of his story. He came back! And his comeback was incredible. He went on to build a company called DaMark, which is one of the largest merchandising companies in the United States.

Or how about a lady I interviewed, Mrs. Doris DeBoe, a ninth grade math teacher who was diagnosed with cancer and given only a few months to live. She was stunned when she got the diagnosis, but made up her mind that she was not going to die. She looked the doctors in their eyes and said, "I am not going to die any time soon. I am going to live for twenty-five more years because I have too many children to teach!" I am glad to say I was able to celebrate her eighty-third birthday with her; and when she passed, she did not die from cancer (she beat cancer four times), instead she died from old age. I spoke at her funeral and we celebrated her life and how she accomplished her goal to beat cancer. She lived for more than twenty-five years after the doctors had given her six months. In my book *A Setback Is a Setup for a Comeback,* I share a powerful quote from Mrs. DeBoe. She said, "Tell the people in your book that I might have cancer, but cancer does not have me! Also tell them that doctors can give you the diagnosis, but God gives you the prognosis!"

I also interviewed a woman who was moving up the corporate ladder, but just before reaching the top she was fired, due to her age. After giving so much to the company, she was devastated when they let her go. Yet, she didn't give up. She kept fighting—and eventually she came back and bought the company!

Throughout the book, I shared story after story of people who had setbacks and turned them into comebacks. And I learned that there was a common thread that was apparent in all the stories. There were four common elements: the power of vision, the power of decision, the power of action, and the power of desire.

1. Focus Your Vision

Where there is no vision, the people perish.
—PROVERBS 29:18 KJV

Where you put your focus and your energy will determine where you will go. If you focus on the setback and the challenges it brought you, you cannot effectively move forward. However, when you focus your vision on what you want to become—despite the setback—then you're using the setback for what it really is: a transition period.

Since we will all go through some sort of change or setback at one time or another, it's important to be able to look past the obstacle and plan your future strategies. To develop your new business focus, ask yourself these questions:

- What is the big picture I have for my future?

- What can I do differently to keep this setback from occurring again?

- What goals (sales, product development, customer retention, etc.) do I want my business to achieve in the next three, six, and twelve months?

- How can I use this setback as a learning experience?

Use the answers to these questions as your guide to develop your new business focus.

2. Make a Decision

Both success and failure are decisions. Once your vision is in place, you need to decide you're going to win despite the setback. The truth is that successful business people choose to be successful. They understand that decision and choice are integral parts of the success formula. No matter what setback they encounter, they decide to overcome it and prevail.

Decisions you will have to make for your business to overcome a setback include:

- *Who are my advisors?* Negative advisors who focus on the setback won't help you overcome it. You need to decide to associate with positive advisors who share your vision.

- *Is my new goal big enough?* Just because you had a setback doesn't mean you have to start over small. Make a decision to see the big picture first. Then you can work your way backward to meeting that goal.

- *What steps must I take to meet my goal?* Plan out and decide specifically what you will do to meet your new goal. For example, if your goal is to increase sales by 33 percent, write out what you will do to accomplish that and the timeframe you're allowing yourself to meet the goal.

3. Take Action

A decision without action is simply an illusion, and an action without a vision is mere confusion. Yet a vision plus decisive action can change the world.

Once you decide on the various factors to making your new business vision a reality, you must take action on each and every one. Unfortunately, many business people never act on their decisions. While they have every intention of making their new business vision a reality, they lack the determination and persistence that comes with taking action.

By taking action on a decision, you're also taking responsibility for the setback. The word decision is taken from the Greek word for "to cut." When you make an incision, you cut "in," and when you make a decision, you cut "off"! Take responsibility and cut off those people, places, and things that will keep you from living your dreams. Once you take responsibility for your actions, you're ready to move forward and attain your next goal. Remember, you might not be responsible for getting knocked down, but you are responsible for getting back up. Only those who act achieve their goals.

4. Keep the Desire

Desire is the degree of energy you're willing to exert to reach your goal. In other words, how badly do you want your business to survive, and what are you willing to do to achieve business success?

Imagine I took you to a major league football stadium and told you that somewhere on that football field, one million dollars was buried—and then I offered you a shovel. Would you be interested in digging? Most people would say, "Yes!" I believe that even though you wouldn't have the first clue about where to start digging or how deep to go, most people would be willing to dig, and dig, for that one million dollars. In fact, on television reality shows, we see lots of people who eat worms and take part in other antics for a chance at a jackpot, so I have to imagine that digging up a football field isn't so bad!

The point is that you are willing to go out and dig with the anticipation that there is a reward for your efforts. You must have the determination to dig and keep fighting for your dreams. You must be determined and persistent to achieve your goals. I believe the same is true for life! There are millions of dollars out in the world with your name on them, waiting for you. But to get the money, you must be determined and persistent—and you must keep digging!

Many people who take action quickly give up because their desire falters. Either a new idea strikes them and they lose focus, or they encounter another minor setback and become discouraged. To reach the new business goal you have set for yourself, you must have the desire to consistently follow through with every action, even if it involves a degree of risk. While taking a risk may be intimidating, especially after a setback, it's a necessary ingredient to reaching your new goal. Turning your setback into a comeback will take initiative and action. And initiative and action always involve risk: no guts, no glory—no risk, no reward! Progress always involves risk. You cannot get to second base if you are afraid to leave first base.

Decide how badly you want to achieve the goal, and then keep going after it until you achieve it. Remember, a setback is not an "if" proposition, it's a "when" proposition. And when one occurs in your life, you need to make a conscious decision to view it not as a problem but as a learning opportunity. You must decide what you're going to do about the setback and focus on the solution.

As I interviewed people for *A Setback Is a Setup for a Comeback,* I found that there was a consistent pattern—Vision, Decision, Action, and Desire—that ran through the stories they told me. I started doing more research on simple steps that could be implemented in our everyday activities to turn our setbacks into comebacks, and I identified a 12-step program for turning your setbacks into comebacks! The 12 steps are:

1. Check your perspective. What you see is what you get! It is not so much that seeing is believing, but rather that believing is the key to eventually seeing!

2. Recognize it's life. Life 101 says, "Some days you're the windshield, and some days you're the bug!" Life happens—setbacks happen to everyone, but it is your attitude that will eventually make the difference.

3. Focus on your goal. If the dream is big enough, the problems don't matter. The bigger the dream, the bigger the reward.

4. Make the tough decisions. Now that you have had a setback, what are you going to do about it? It is not so much what happens to you, but what you do about it that counts!

5. Decide to stay positive. Positive people tend to live longer and tend to enjoy the journey much more!

6. Stop and think. Step back, look in, check out, and think up! Look at all your options. You

always have options, but the key to success is to make wise choices.

7. Take action. You can have lights and cameras, but nothing happens until you take action! Many talk about living their dreams, but only those who act on their dreams are able to make them into realities.

8. Take responsibility. Face it, trace it, erase it, and replace it. First, face the problem. Then, trace the problem and learn from it, erase the problem—don't dwell on it. Finally, replace the problem—replace the negative in your life with something positive and inspiring.

9. Harness your anger. Use it for good! Anger is the word danger without the "d." The d is for discipline! Anger is a natural emotion—the key is to be disciplined.

10. Have faith, and remind yourself that you are blessed and highly favored! Positive, courageous faith can give you power for the toughest journeys.

11. Affirm to win, refuse to lose, and never give up! Never, ever, ever give up! Winners never quit and quitters never win!

12. Have an attitude of gratitude! Learn to find the blessings in every burden. Be grateful for each and every day!

Every successful person has had setbacks; however, he or she realizes that a setback is not the end of the road, but rather a bend in the road...and the only ones who crash are those who fail to make the turn. When you view your setback as a chance for future growth, every challenge can have a positive outcome, and every personal setback can eventually be seen as nothing but a setup for an incredible comeback.

ARE YOU SERIOUS?

I received a note from an old friend from my time as a nightclub singer. He said he had seen me on television and wanted to know what I did to change my life. I told him that when I was fired from the nightclub—which I had built into one of the top nightclubs in Washington, DC, because it was more cost effective to buy a karaoke machine than pay a band—I decided to change...and as Jim Rohn says, "Once you change, everything changes for you!"

I told him I made a commitment to grow and to expand my thinking. I started a course of self-development and made a commitment to read books with a positive message, listen to motivational tapes, and attend lots of motivational seminars and rallies. In short, I told him that I decided to get serious about my success. I made up my mind that I was going to do whatever was necessary to develop myself and grow into a person who was ready for success. I remember Les Brown telling me once that most people are "seriously, not serious about success." He said they talk about it, and talk about it, and talk about it, but never do anything about it. So I made up my mind to get serious!

I made a commitment to get up early and stay up late; I made a commitment to read everything I could about self-development. I turned off the television and heavily invested my time in books and audios. I made the commitment to get on the phone and make sales calls. I would get on the phone early in the morning and would continue until late into the evening, and when I got tired and wanted to stop, I would always make one more call. I made a commitment that on a daily basis I would do more than I was paid to do, and give more than I was expected to give, and go further than I was asked to go. And I have found it to be true that if you do more than you are paid to do, then one day, you will be paid more than you do. And if you do the things today that others won't do, you will have the things tomorrow that others won't have.

My old friend then asked me what three things I do on a daily basis. I told him that I start each day the same way, with prayer and meditation. I thank God for each morning as I get out of bed and I proudly proclaim, "This is the day that the Lord has made, and I am glad and rejoice in it!" I have an attitude of gratitude, because I have another opportunity to go out and live my dream!

Second, I ask myself, *Willie, what would you do today if you were serious?* Once I get the answers, I write them down and get to work on making my dreams into realities. Then I ask myself, *What can I do today to get better?* I have learned that success is the result of personal and professional development and that getting better requires daily development. Greatness at any task does not happen in a day, but rather day by day. It is the daily regimen that makes the difference. Just like you grow your muscles little by little, so too, do you grow yourself and your success little by little, day by day.

I told my friend that this was not rocket science, but it did take a PHD—Persistence, Hunger, and Determination! Most of all, it takes a commitment to grow ourselves so we can grow our futures. Then we must make a commitment to that commitment! In this book, I will help you focus on the question: *Are you serious?*

Every successful businessperson has had setbacks; however, they realize that a setback is not the end of the road, but rather a bend in the road...and the only ones who crash are those who fail to make the turn. By viewing your business's setback as a chance for future growth, every business challenge can have a positive outcome, and every setback can be seen as nothing but a setup for an incredible comeback.

The question that constantly is asked during tough times is, "How in the world do we survive this ordeal?" There are no easy answers, but there are concepts that have been time-tested and solutions that work. These concepts worked in the 1930s and have worked throughout the other recessions and tough economic times we have seen; they will work for you today, as well. In fact, we have seen that many of the same tendencies exist today as there were in years past. Movie studios have seen the highest ticket sales ever in the midst of recessions and tough economic times, and companies that specialize in home theater and home entertainment see incredible increases in sales during tough times; people feel they cannot afford outside entertainment, so they pay to be able to stay home. It is during these times when you can use your creativity to build great wealth. Yet these principles only work if you are willing to work them, and you are willing to diligently apply them to your life.

Warren Buffett, who was recently listed as one of the wealthiest men in the world, said that recessions are very challenging times, yet are also a great time to create wealth. He actually calls it "an economic Pearl Harbor," which is a time when everything appears to be blown apart, yet from that challenge beautiful plants will sprout. Mr. Buffett said that recessions and economic downturns are circular in nature— they have come before and will probably come again in our lifetimes. He also said we should learn from history. We have seen worse economic situations, and each one ended and the economy bounced back better than it had been before. He said with each recovery, the best days are truly ahead for those who are willing to think differently and not buy into negative commentaries and negative outlooks. Mr. Buffett feels that the economic downturns offer great opportunities to those who have a positive outlook and have made up their mind not to follow the crowd of negative thinkers.

In an interview on CNBC, Warren Buffett said, "The bad news creates fear and anxiety, but you must fight the fear and realize that everything will be all right in time. The free enterprise system works! Occasionally the machine gets gummed up, but it will right itself and you can trust that the system works!" After he spoke on the subject of banking and savings, saying that the best days were ahead for the banking industry, the stock prices for Wells Fargo bank rose more than 24 percent!

Mr. Buffett also advised his listeners not to get caught up in the fear and panic, but rather look to the future with optimism and excitement, and look for opportunities that are all around. Finally, he said, "When other people were greedy (during the Internet boom and eventual bust), that was when I was laid back! But when the others were fearful, then that was when I was greedy!"

I agree with Warren Buffett: A time of economic downturns is when we should examine the patterns that existed in the past, while looking optimistically to the future. It is the time to look for opportunities and look at possibilities and be bold. Those who think differently and open their eyes to the opportunities and possibilities are those who will prosper. Jack Adgate wrote, "What does every recession have in common? They all ended with very different results for businesses. At the end of the 1990 recession, Walmart had pulled ahead of Sears, Gillette beat Colgate-Palmolive, and Merrill Lynch beat Bear Stearns." History has proven it is the same for each recession or depression, as well as your personal history—if you don't give up, you can turn your setbacks into greenbacks.

The main question is whether you see a setback (such as a recession or a personal economic downturn) as a hopeless problem or as a strategic opportunity? What do you want your life and business to look like once you've overcome the setback?

In changing and challenging times, I believe it is necessary to think differently! If you are willing to do different things and do some things differently, you will see positive changes. In this book I share ideas and strategies that will help you to think differently and help you prosper. These ideas will help you to thrive, not just survive, and help you turn any economic setback into greenbacks!

THE ROAD LESS TRAVELED

As we grow older, we live through one challenging experience after another. As M. Scott Peck stated in the first line of his landmark book, *The Road Less Traveled,* "Life is difficult." Period! He's right, life is difficult. Life is challenging. And there are times when life is downright unfair. Yet life is still worth living. Even with the challenges and the difficulties we all must endure, life still is a beautiful thing! I have a sign on my desk that states, "Life does not have to be perfect to be wonderful!"

Through the years, I have often heard older folks say, "If you have not had tough times in your life, then just keep living!" We all have some tough times and will eventually have some setbacks in our lives. We will all experience some challenging times, yet there are great opportunities in the midst of the challenges. We will have some times of crisis, but we must understand the true definition of crisis to see the possibilities for our futures.

We constantly hear that we are in the midst of a crisis. I do not disagree that we are in the midst of a crisis, but I disagree with the way that crisis is defined. We typically think of *crisis* as a calamity, a time of hurt, pain, and despair. Yes, during this tough time, there are times of hurt, pain, and despair, but those challenges are not the totality of the situation. The word *crisis* is an interesting word because it has dual attributes: great challenge and difficulty, yet at the same time great opportunity! Napoleon Hill stated in his well-known book, *Think and Grow Rich,* "In every adversity there is always the seed for equal or greater benefit." In that spirit, let me share a few ideas that I believe will help you to get through any crisis and come out on the other side greater and better than you began!

As we get into the specific steps of this economic comeback, my goal is to give you specific strategies on how to not only survive, but to thrive through challenging times.

Warren Buffett was right: Now is the time! It is setbacks into greenbacks time! We will get through this! It's comeback time! Get ready for your incredible comeback! Get ready to turn this economic setback into greenbacks! Let's make it happen!

And now, on to the *seven steps to turn setbacks into greenbacks!*

MAKE UP YOUR MIND: GET PRESSED, BUT DO NOT PANIC

(Because Pressure Makes Diamonds, but Panic Makes Disasters)

"Tough times don't last but tough people do!"
—DR. ROBERT SCHULLER

Challenges with money happen to everyone at some time or another. I know it's not fun. In fact, I know it's quite the opposite—painful. When we experience an economic setback, whether personally or on a grander scale, we tend to get that uncomfortable feeling of losing control, which can shake our equilibrium and is a feeling that no one likes. Often that lack of control is accompanied by an increased level of pressure and anxiety. When you're broke, busted, and disgusted, it's hard to concentrate and see a future where money isn't short and paying bills isn't so difficult. I like the way my friend Dr. Beecher Hicks says it, "The pressure gets stronger when money gets funny, and change gets strange!" Yet the good news, the really good news, is that there is a solution to this problem, and it starts with your thinking!

FIRST AND FOREMOST, MAKE UP YOUR MIND

I have been through the pressure of tough economic times before, and I learned some valuable lessons in the process. I learned that pressure actually can make diamonds in your life, but it is critical that when the pressure comes your way, you make up your mind to use the pressure to make you stronger and better, not make you weaker and bitter. Start thinking differently. Think positively and concentrate on what you want, rather than what you don't want and what you fear. Why? Because whatever you focus on longest becomes strongest!

Developing a winning mindset is crucial. The first step to turn a setback into greenbacks is to make up your mind! Make up your mind that you will win, somehow, someway, and that when the dust clears you will still be standing. It is like in the movie *The Color Purple* when Miss Celie decides to leave her mean, abusive husband, Mister. When she tells him she is going to leave, he begins to tell her that no one wants her, that she is ugly, and that she has never done anything of any worth. She looks at him with steely confidence and says, "I might be ugly, and I might not have done anything of any worth in your eyes...but I'm still here! I'm still here!" It was a declaration of achievement and a statement of worth! So, the first step to turn a setback into greenbacks is to make up your mind! To win in life and business, you must make up your mind—you must make the commitment that you are willing to go beyond your comfort zone. Once you make up your mind and make the commitment, you must be willing to keep working toward your goal until you reach it.

As with most things in life, the first step is always the most critical. The making up of the mind is the first important step in this equation. Most people do not win in life because they don't make up their minds and don't commit themselves to the goal. Goethe said, "Until one is committed there is hesitancy, the chance to draw back, always ineffectiveness. But the minute, the moment one definitely commits oneself, that is the moment that Providence (the hand of God) moves also. All manner of things occur that would never regularly have occurred. Boldness has magic and genius in it, begin it now!"

If you want to get on the winner's track, the first step is to make up your mind, because nothing in life is more important than a made-up mind.

Most people have an "I hope I can" mindset. But a person who has a made-up mind has an "I know I can! I know I will!" mindset. These are the people who consistently seem to win in life and in business. They consistently beat the odds and continue to have success. They go through the tough economic times and come out on the other end better and wealthier. We know that stormy economic winds are going to blow, but if we have made up our minds that we are going to win, we find that we are on the right path to greater success.

Some years ago I was asked by Microsoft to initiate their new Web Meetings portal for the product kick-off program. While I was asked to head the Web Meetings portal, Donald

Trump was asked to kick off the business development portal. As a result of this program, I was introduced to the Trump team. I had a chance to learn more about Donald Trump and his thinking, and why he continued to succeed even in challenging times. And one of the reasons for his consistent success is the way he thinks. I learned that Donald Trump thinks he will win even when all the odds are stacked against him. He has a made-up mind and does not allow doubt or fear to creep into his thinking or limit his options.

Mr. Trump states that he faced repeated opposition when he first came to Manhattan to seek new projects to develop. It was a bad time for the real estate market in New York, and it was a bad economy, yet he made up his mind that this was really an opportunity. And as a result of his thinking, he was able to overcome the fear that kept others from acting during dire economic times. Most people were planning to wait until the economy turned around, but Mr. Trump decided that this was the time to move, and that he was going to be successful, come hell or high water.

Once he made up his mind, he went to work on the challenges that faced him, and he eventually succeeded with that project. Since those early ventures, he has had one challenging project after another, and even had a time in the 1980s when the market went down and many of the banks called in their loans. But Mr. Trump again made up his mind. He decided to think outside the box and came up with a series of creative loan restructuring programs that would get everyone paid but would buy him time to get it done. He was able to succeed in those ventures as well, which led to more deals and more celebrity. Why? Because he made up his mind to win! I want you to make up your mind and get in the habit of going after success!

Once you make up your mind, you are halfway there—the battle is half-won. Very little actually happens until you make up your mind. Make up your mind that you will not just survive your present situation but thrive! Make up your mind that you will find a way to succeed! Once you make up your mind, what follows becomes a whole lot easier. Very little actually happens until you make up your mind! Make up your mind that you will develop your will to win! It is not only important, it is critical. Make up your mind—in fact, do it right now!

You must make up your mind—you must make the commitment that you are willing to go beyond your comfort zone. Once you make up your mind and make the commitment, you must be willing to keep working toward your goal until you reach it.

You must convince yourself that you are going to succeed! Say it out loud! It has been said that half the battle is the mental struggle that we wage within ourselves. Today you will find a way to succeed! You will begin to develop your will to win! It is not only important, it is critical. Make up your mind...right now!

MINDSET IMPACTS WEALTH

Not only is your mindset the driving force that starts you on your journey, but it is also critically important in the process of creating wealth, especially in the midst of financial challenges. It all depends on your mindset and your level of determination. You are going to have to be determined to achieve it!

People often confuse determination and persistence because they are so similar, but persistence is an action, while determination is an attitude. When the two combine, dreams become realities! If you want to be a success, you must have a dream, you must decide to follow that dream, and you must make a determined decision that you will keep going until you achieve that dream, whatever it takes—you must keep going until you achieve it!

I am often asked about the title of my first book, *It Only Takes a Minute to Change Your Life*, and whether you can really change your life in a minute. I always say, "Absolutely!" You can definitely change your life in a minute. The minute you make a decision and move in a new direction is the minute you change your life. You might not reach your destination in a minute, but you certainly can change your direction in minute. And the minute you make up your mind and move in that new direction, you absolutely change your life. The same is true for turning your setbacks into greenbacks—you must first make up your mind!

GET PRESSED, BECAUSE PRESSURE MAKES DIAMONDS!

Pressure is a word we all know and a feeling we typically do not like to experience. Most people experience pressure in some form on a daily basis. The pressure to do well at the office; the pressure of dealing with traffic and getting to and from work; we experience manifold pressures in our daily lives. Over time, we usually adjust to the pressures, and most times we learn to handle them. Yet there is something different about financial pressure. Financial pressure can shake our equilibrium. Financial pressure, unchecked, can make you crazy. Yet it is exactly that financial pressure that can be the spark to your developing wealth. It is the pressure that makes diamonds, and can develop a diamond mine for you.

In conversations with my son and his friends, they often use the word *pressed*. In most circles, getting pressed is not seen as something cool. Some believe that it smacks of desperation. Yet I contend that it is not a matter of being cool but rather a matter of being focused and determined to win. I contend that being pressed and being desperate are two completely different things.

To be pressed is a time of being intense, focused, and determined to win. To be desperate means that you are scattered and are grasping for straws, while drowning in a sea of uncertainty. A pressure makes diamonds, while desperation leads to panic and panic leads to disaster. I believe it is necessary and wise to recognize the importance and the power of being pressed. To be pressed is to be in a state in which we are focused and totally committed to achieving our goals. It is a time when we move beyond a casual interest in achieving our goals and step up to a level of total commitment in which we are absolutely determined to reach our goals. My friend Les Brown says, "If you are casual, you will become a casualty!" I am confident that you must make the decision to move beyond the casual level and get serious, get focused, and get pressed! In tough times, you must step up your game and step up your level of commitment. If you do, you will astound yourself with what you are able to accomplish.

To panic means to take action without thinking or having a rational plan. To be pressed means to work harder and to work smarter, with a higher level of purpose and conviction. I like to say that pressure creates diamonds, while panic creates disasters! It is okay—in fact it is advisable—to have times when you are pressed and determined to achieve your goals, but it is a mistake to panic. When people are pressed, they raise their level of activity and intensity, but what is important is *how* they raise their intensity level. Some people handle pressure by reacting in a negative way, while others handle pressure by responding in a positive manner. The clear difference is that one is negative and the other is positive.

When you *respond* to an issue, there is a positive movement, so the impact of the stimulus is positive. The opposite is true with a *reaction;* there is a negative movement, so the impact of the stimulus is negative. Let's say that a friend of yours has an illness and you take him or her to the hospital. The person is admitted, and the doctor prescribes a medication to treat the illness. Later, when you visit and ask the doctor how your friend is doing, if the doctor says your friend *reacted* to the medication, you immediately know that it is not good news. Yet if the doctor says your friend *responded* to the medication, then you know that it is working and your friend is doing better.

The ability to respond rather than react can be learned. The difference rests primarily in how you perceive and look at life—in other words, it is primarily about your attitude. Far too often people react to situations and panic, rather than respond and stay calm. I recommend you respond and stay calm. Practice calmness and stay focused. Be pressed in turning your setbacks into greenbacks, but do not panic!

Pressure creates greater focus and clarity. Great athletes get pressed and get focused if they are behind in the closing minutes of a contest. They focus and they do not panic. Joe

Montana was one of the greatest quarterbacks to play American football. He was the leader of the Super Bowl-winning San Francisco 49ers football team. He was often called "The king of the two-minute drill!" If his team was behind in the last two minutes, he would calmly gather his troops and tell them to focus and get ready for a two-minute war.

Michael Jordan was another athlete who did not panic and was known for his ability to focus. Michael Jordan was the leader of the Chicago Bulls basketball team and was known as someone who became a world champion as a result of his ability to focus. At the end of the game when the Bulls were behind in the score and someone needed to step up and make some points, Michael Jordan always wanted the ball. He did not panic; he pressed and he pushed himself to perform at the next level. Winners decide to win and choose not to panic and fall apart; they press and focus all their energies on winning. Are you ready to get through the tough economic times and win? Are you ready to go to war and win? Are you pressed, yet refuse to panic? I hope so, because there is no power in a panic!

So, how do you turn that financial pressure into opportunities for greater success and into situations to your advantage? Glad you asked. Just as the earth's pressure can transform a piece of coal into a priceless diamond, so too can the pressures of life transform your situation into a diamond. Pressure makes diamonds, but it is critical that you use the pressure for your good, not for your destruction. Remember, pressure makes diamonds, but panic makes destruction.

It is critical that you are focused and determined, pressed to succeed, yet you must not panic! You must not panic because it robs you of your ability to think clearly and exercise all your options. You need to have the right mindset to consider all your options. Panic detracts from that. And if you cannot select from a clear set of options, your chance of making a *great* choice declines significantly.

Once panic sets in, not only do people tend to make poor choices, they also tend to follow the lead of others who are making poor choices as well.

During the U.S. stock market crash of 1929, thousands of people panicked, and it became mass hysteria. It was an epidemic of poor choices and bad decisions. People jumped off buildings and took guns and committed suicide. But, in the end, the market came back, bigger and better than before.

I was amazed at how people panicked when the stock market tanked in our time. Some people who held stock that had a high of $65 a share panicked when the market fell and hit bottom at $1.05 a share, and they sold their stock at the bottom. Why would anyone sell it then? I have always been told that the secret to success in the stock market is to buy low and sell high. If you didn't sell it when it first started to fall, why in the world would you sell at the bottom? Many people panicked and sold their stock at the bottom...and then the stock rose again! So, back to that fundamental first step of making up your mind: make up your mind *not* to panic. There is no power in panic.

THE REALITIES OF RECESSION

The reality of recession and other economic downturns is that they will come and they will go. Recessions and economic downturns are a part of life, and if we live long enough we will see, from time to time, the economy struggle. Similarly, we will occasionally have personal recessions...which means we run out of money. We occasionally will see our personal economic status fluctuate. It is a part of the journey of life, and once you have learned to successfully navigate the economic storms, you will come to the realization that a recession is not something to be feared but rather something to be managed.

First, let's look at what a recession is all about. A recession is a general slump in business and an increase in unemployment. It's important to note that both a recession and a depression are economic situations that start with fluctuations in the economic condition of a country or group of countries and then is fueled by fear (corporate fear and then fear of consumers to spend money), which leads to lower sales and eventually to job losses. The cycle keeps going until there is a reduction of fear and more money is pushed into the system.

Since the Great Depression, there have been 11 serious recessions and economic downturns, yet in each of those recessions and economic downturns there were people who emerged as millionaires. How did they do it? How can you do it?

Let's start with taking a look at a few people who became rich as a result of a recession or economic downturn.

Michael J. Cullen

Michael J. Cullen created a new concept called the supermarket during the Great Depression. He moved people away from mom-and-pop grocery stores to a place where they could get everything they wanted under one roof, usually for better prices. He saw an opportunity to help people save money and time, and he prospered during the worst economic situation the United States has ever seen by thinking and coming up with something that helps people be more successful. His motto was "Pile it high: sell it cheap."

Charles Darrow

You might not know Charles Darrow's name, but you certainly know his invention. He created a little game called *Monopoly* that we still play today. He lost everything in the crash of 1929, but refused to give up and throw in the towel. He worked on an idea for a new board game to help people feel like they were rich. Within a year of the game being released, it sold more than 20,000 units and Darrow became a multimillionaire.

J. Paul Getty

J. Paul Getty used money he received in an inheritance to buy oil stocks after the stock market crash, when the prices were low. He then held them and sold them for a big profit when prices started to rise. He became a billionaire because he was smart and did what we are all told to do with investments—buy low and sell high!

Howard Hughes

Howard Hughes was a daredevil aviator who took his risk-taking skills to the next level after the stock market crash of 1929. He went on to make films, because he figured people would be willing to pay the price of a movie ticket to escape the gloom and doom of everyday life. He was absolutely right! Then, in the mid-1930s, he thought that people would want to travel once the recession was over, so he started Hughes Aircraft Company and positioned himself as the king of aircraft. Howard Hughes saw a need and took a chance on his vision for the future.

For those of us who were born after the Great Depression, the latest recession has been an interesting lesson in human nature. We have seen people turn from record spending and record credit and debt levels to a change in habits and even a cultural change. We have seen venerable institutional companies like Lehman Brothers go out of business or be bought by their competitors. We have seen companies that were part of our landscape disappear overnight. We have seen people lose their life savings and their long-term investments. We have seen record foreclosures and distress sales. We have seen people lose their jobs, and many of them are unable to find another job for months and months.

We all know people who have been personally affected and we feel pain for them. It's only natural to hear the daily reports about the bad times and secretly wonder how it will affect us. It can create a malaise that settles over a community, a city, a state, and even a country! But this is not the time to throw our hands in the air and give up; rather, this is a time to look up, think up, and come up with new ideas and strategies to turn this economic setback into a comeback!

We have seen tough times before, and we have come out of each one bigger and better and stronger than we were before the challenge. In each tough situation, people have discovered some specific keys to winning. Even in tough times, there are some who are able to turn the sour lemon of an economy into lemonade. There are some who are about to see the seeds of opportunity in the midst of adversity. Napoleon Hill, the author of the landmark book *Think and Grow Rich*, said, "Every ADVERSITY, every failure, every heartache, carries with it the seeds of an equal or greater opportunity!"

LESSONS FROM THE VOICE
OF EXPERIENCE

I have found that there are some people who have discovered how to get though tough economic times and come out better than they began. I have had the pleasure of interviewing a good number of individuals who have discovered the secret for coming out of tough economic times better on my SiriusXM Radio show, *The Willie Jolley Wealthy Ways Radio Show.* This show features ideas and insights from some of the world's best and brightest on the topic of success and wealth building. David Yoho, one of my past interviewees, is a legend in the motivational speaking industry. He is a world-renowned speaker and business consultant who travels across the country sharing his ideas. Even though he is an octogenarian, (someone well past the age of 80), he has the passion and energy of someone half his age, and is one of the wisest men I have had the pleasure to interview.

Born in the 1920s, David vividly remembers the stock market crash of 1929 and growing up through that Great Depression. During the interview, he spoke of the important economic lessons he learned in his 80-plus years, such as the fact that world economies will have good times, followed by tough times; followed by good times, followed by tough times; and then back to good times! Those who succeed over the long term realize that this "came to pass...it did not come to stay." Those who understand that setbacks are simply part of the business process are those who thrive; while those who dwell on the changes setbacks bring, routinely falter. David said, "I grew up in a time when we didn't know anything but tough times. We learned that tough times don't last, but tough people do. You must not panic, but keep working on your goals. You can get through these tough times by making a commitment to personal achievement!"

The fact is that setbacks are really simply a part of life, and in life things change—the secret is to not give up! Keep going and keep growing through the challenges. No matter what industry you're in, you're bound to have things change. The key is to remember that these temporary setbacks can empower you to reach even greater levels of business success.

As I have talked to other people old enough to remember the Great Depression, they all say that tough times are a part of life, but we can get through them if we understand the principles. It is not a possibility, but a reality of life. Therefore, it is critical to think through the problem and not to panic.

HOW TO DEVELOP THE POWER OF CALM

Some years ago, there was a deodorant commercial on television that stated that those who are most successful learned to stay cool, calm, and collected. I have to think that message is intended for a lot more than just deodorant. You have a choice when life starts to get crazy: you can get crazy with it, or you can remain calm. The choices you make will have consequences that either help you or hurt you.

I have learned that although many people are aware that it is not good to panic, they continue to panic in the moments of challenge. This is because they do not know how to be calm. Remaining calm in the face of turmoil is a conscious decision, and it must be developed like any other skill. Those who develop the ability to maintain calm in crisis moments are those who have the greatest amount of success.

Captain Chesley "Sully" Sullenberger became an international hero because of his ability to remain calm in the midst of potential disaster. He was the pilot of the doomed US Airways plane that lost both engines after being hit by a flock of birds while taking off from LaGuardia Airport in New York City. As he flew over Manhattan, he realized he had no engines and no place to land the plane, so he calmly decided to get the plane past Manhattan and try to land it in the Hudson River. He was able to do this successfully, saving the lives of all 155 passengers onboard. *The Wall Street Journal* reported that this was first time in 50 years of commercial jet flight that a pilot was able to successfully execute one of the most technically challenging maneuvers—landing a jetliner in water—without loss of life or major injuries.

I had the opportunity to share the stage with Captain Sullenberger and he said that the first thing he did when he realized he had lost all engines was to decide not to panic and to stay calm and focus his energies. He thought about his options, and when he realized he could not get back to the airport, he decided to land the plane in the water. He said that he "forced himself" to remain calm, because it was only with a calm mind that he would be able to pull off this kind of operation. Many of the people on the plane and their families met with Captain Sullenberger a few weeks after the crash and thanked him profusely for saving their lives and their loved ones. He was humbled by the adulation and the comments, but he said that the key was a decision to remain calm and to think positively and look at the possibilities. Then it became a matter of turning those possibilities into realities. Force yourself to remain calm and think about your possibilities, and then go about turning *your* possibilities into realities.

THINK UP THEN SPEAK UP, TALK TO YOURSELF, AND TALK POWER INTO YOUR SITUATION

Most people do not realize the power of positive self-talk. First you must think up, which is to focus on positive, uplifting thoughts. After you think up, then you can go to the next level, which is to speak up. To speak up is to consciously have positive self-talk with yourself. It might sound a bit silly, but most people have an ongoing internal conversation with themselves that is negative. Yet, those who learn to have positive talk tend to win more! Speak goodness into your life and learn to speak power into your situation. For years I have used this technique to calm myself in the midst of challenging situations. I have found that my own words can give comfort to my mind and my spirit. I make a point of saying to myself, "Stay calm! Stay calm! This is not a big deal! Everything will be all right, just stay calm!" It sounds so simple, yet it is so very effective. I recommend that you simply try it; you will see that this works. And the more you practice speaking calm into your life, the more you are able to handle challenging situations. Try it for yourself, you will be amazed!

SPEAK POSITIVITY INTO YOUR SITUATION

There will be times when you must use your faith to get to the solution. I believe it is important to learn to speak positivity into your challenges and situations. I've had moments in my life when the circumstances were totally out of my control. At those times, I spoke about my faith and my expectations, and I found that this brought calm into my life and calm into the situation.

For example, once, years ago, I took my mother to get a manicure. While I was waiting, one of the other manicurists convinced me to get my nails cut and buffed. Part of her process was to take hand lotion and massage each hand before cutting the nails. She told me that I needed to remove my marriage band, but I resisted because we had just celebrated our tenth wedding anniversary, and my wife and I had given each other special matching rings. The manicurist insisted on having me take off the ring, and she went about putting the lotion on my hands and giving them a good once over. As she was finishing, my mother said she needed to go to another appointment. I quickly got up and paid and helped my mother to the car. Of course, I forgot my new wedding anniversary ring!

When I got home, I remembered the ring and tried to call the salon, but it had closed. All I could think about was that I had left the ring on the counter and there were a number of people in line after me, and I began to feel nervous, thinking that one of those people might have accidentally picked up my ring. The more I thought about it, the worse it got in my mind. I got to a point where I started to panic, but then I realized that panic was not a healthy response to this situation. I started to speak to myself, and said, "Do not worry! Remember Willie, you are blessed and highly favored! All will be well!" I said that over and over again, and went to bed that night using that statement as a mantra: "Do not worry! Remember Willie, you are blessed and highly favored! All will be well!"

The next morning, I went to the salon when it opened and quickly ran to the counter where I had placed my ring—but it was not there. I looked for the lady who had done my nails, but she had not arrived yet. I felt panic trying to get hold of me, but I decided to keep speaking calm into this situation. I continued to repeat my mantra. When the manicurist from the day before walked into the salon, I ran up to her and told her about how I'd left my ring on the counter. She looked at me and asked me to sit down. She then opened her top desk drawer and said, "Here you are! I put it away for you. I didn't have your number, so I couldn't call you, but I put it safely away for you. I could tell it was important to you, and I wanted to make sure you got it back!" I hugged her and thanked her, and I made a note to remind myself to always remain calm and learn to speak good into life and into challenging situations!

THIS TOO SHALL PASS

Throughout the Bible, we see the phrase *it came to pass*, which usually implies that an event or experience came to fulfillment. Yet there is another meaning that I believe is just as powerful in light of these tough times and the numerous challenges associated with them. It means that this situation did not come to stay but rather it came to pass, to move by quickly.

Economic storms, like thunderstorms, come into our lives at various times, but you need to stay mindful of the fact that they come to pass, they do not come to stay—and I have been known to exclaim in tough times that "this too shall pass!" I say to you, do not panic and do not jump off any bridges, because this too shall pass. This too shall pass!

MAKE GOOD CHOICES

My friend Donald Cooper, a speaker and trainer from Canada, told me a story that his dad used to tell him. His dad told him to be willing to go through the hedge to get to the other side. In the process there would be scratches and discomfort, but once you made it through the hedge to the other side, there would be amazing sights and sounds that could not be experienced before going through the hedge. If you make poor choices and don't look to the future with high hopes and high expectations, then you will not position yourself for the amazing things that are possible for the future. Unfortunately, many people panic and make poor decisions and turn small molehills into major mountains that haunt them for years to come. And some make an even worse decision—ending their lives, and in doing so they make a permanent decision for a temporary problem. Never give up on life because you are in the midst of a storm—the sun will shine again! This storm too shall pass!

BURNT BUT BLESSED— LEARN TO STAY CALM

There are times when life gets hectic and crazy. But because life is crazy does not mean you must get crazy with it! Those who win in life are those who are able to stay calm in the midst of life's craziness. The more you practice staying calm, the more you will stay calm in a moment of crisis.

I had a moment of crisis when my car caught on fire. I had traveled to Wisconsin and Minnesota to speak. My wife, Dee, chose not to travel with me, because she was attending a women's retreat in Virginia. She also had to teach our communication skills class that Sunday. She had driven her late-model Mercedes to Williamsburg, Virginia, and back to Washington, DC. She picked me up from the airport on Monday. We went to the resort at National Harbor, Maryland, for an afternoon program. After the program, we decided to stop by our church for the last part of Bible study. After Bible study, while I was speaking to the pastor, someone rushed in and said, "Willie, your car is on fire!" We rushed to the parking lot, and sure enough, our car was ablaze.

According to the police, my wife's car had started smoking. Then sparks and flames began to come out from under the hood, as well as the dashboard. The police called the fire department. Since the electrical system was burned and disabled, they could not open the doors or the hood of the car. They had to use an axe to break open the windows and to get the hood open to put out the fire.

As we stood there, watching our car being consumed by flames, someone asked how we were doing. I said, "I am blessed and grateful! This is nothing but a minor setback; and a setback is nothing but a setup for a comeback!"

"You really believe that stuff you talk about, don't you?" he asked. My reply was, "You are absolutely right! This is not a big deal. See, this car could have caught fire while Dee was driving to her conference, to our class, to pick me up from the airport, to take me to my program, or while we were driving to church tonight! I am blessed and so very grateful. And, I know the world will not end. It is just a car. I can replace a car. I can't replace my wife!"

People were amazed that I was so calm. But what they did not know is that I *learned* to stay calm and not let external issues disrupt my internal joy and peace. Happiness is typically a result of the "happenings" in your life. But joy is the result of your internal positioning, and I decided long ago that I would not let "stuff" steal or disrupt my joy!

You, too, can develop calmness within, even in the midst of crazy times. How? One technique is to make a commitment to say calming things to yourself. Practice being calm by saying aloud, "Stay calm, and do not panic!" Then ask yourself, *Will the world stop turning because of this problem?* If the answer is no, keep moving!

By the way, I want to tell you the rest of the story. I truly believe a setback is nothing but a setup for a comeback, and you must keep calm and keep the faith. As I told you, our car was a late-model Mercedes, and when I told the folks at Mercedes what had happened, they went to work and delivered a special edition Mercedes for us that was much nicer and had more bells and whistles than our original vehicle. That is why you must not panic nor lose heart, because a setback is truly a setup for a comeback!

SETTLE DOWN AND THINK UP

When life throws us curveballs, they can come in a wave and they can certainly create waves in their wake. Once the rush of activity begins, we can easily get caught up in the activity, and if we are not mindful, we can get caught up in the mob mentality, the hysteria of the moment. These are times when people get caught up in activities without really thinking it through, yet they do them anyway, because everyone else is doing them.

It typically happens in a rushing wave, in which people act before they think. When a herd stampedes, it's because each cow is carried along with the crowd. We have seen soccer mobs exhibit crazy behavior and fight each other over stupid stuff, and later have no idea why they did what they did. They cannot explain it, they only can describe that it was "so quick that I didn't know what was happening! I just got caught up!"

That is exactly why it is important to stay calm, even when others around you are losing their minds. Keep in mind that someone else's crazy does not have to become your crazy. I make a point of practicing calm even when the people around me are getting overly excited about the issues that are swirling around and about them. Stay calm!

DEVELOP A SOUND MIND

For God has not given us a spirit of fear, but of
power and love and of a sound mind!
—2 TIMOTHY 1:6

Talk yourself into a calm, controlled state of thinking and acting. Develop a calm, composed, sound mind. And whatever you do, remember that God has blessed you with life, power, the ability to love, and the option of maintaining a sound, calm mind. Remember, remaining calm is a choice...so I recommend you use it and not lose it.

Talk to yourself, and learn to talk yourself into a calm and controlled way of thinking and acting. It is critical that you do not lose your composure, because once you've lost your composure, you have lost the battle!

BROKE, BUSTED, AND DISGUSTED

When we are broke, everything becomes magnified. Our molehill-size problems become mountains, and our pains become more pronounced. We can go from broke to busted to plain old disgusted. And we know that tough times can affect people in many different ways. When people lose their jobs, their homes, or their life savings, they also lose their sense of personal security. I have found that when I begin to feel overwhelmed by the state of current affairs, or when I am hit with personal problems that can have an impact on my sanity, I need to step back and recover so that I can get back into the fight.

First, let me say that success is a fight. It is not going to be easy; if it were easy, everyone would do it. Someone said that in life you have a problem, just left a problem, or are on your way to a problem. Life is challenging, yet it is worth the fight!

What should you do if you are depressed? First, you need to determine if your depression is chemical or emotional. A chemical depression needs to be addressed by a medical professional, because it is a medical issue and needs medical attention. Yet some depression is the result of emotional distress due to the effect of overwhelming negative information, our psyche, and our perspective of the world. Studies have shown that a constant barrage of negative input can alter our emotional state and our outlook on life. We have all experienced a tough day when "Murphy" comes to visit (you know Murphy's Law: Anything that can go wrong will go wrong, at the worst possible time). When you have those moments, I recommend you make a decision to respond to the feelings and move on them, before they move on you.

When life throws you serious setbacks and depression tries to overtake you, it is critical that you reframe your thinking. The following are a few simple steps that I recommend: change your environment; reframe your thinking with an attitude of gratitude; think about helping others; change your input; fill yourself with the pure, the powerful, and the positive; and rest and rejuvenate.

Change Your Environment

Leave the place where you are, and change the texture of the environment. Maybe you can take a walk, take a drive, or go to a different area of your house or building. The key is to change the input of the moment and get some new input and new perspective. The change can have a tremendous effect on your emotions.

A few years ago when my aunt Eunice died, I started to feel a sense of depression come over me. Aunt Eunice was like a second mother to me; when my mom died after a long illness, Aunt Eunice became a surrogate mother. I talked to her every week. When she died, it hit me pretty hard, and I realized I needed to reframe my thinking. So I told my staff I would be back, and I went for a nice long ride in my car through a park near my office. As I noticed the beautiful scenery, I had a conversation with myself, and asked myself the questions that I often share with families who lose loved ones: "Are you going to curse because a rose bush has thorns? Or are you going to celebrate because a thorn bush has roses? Are you going to curse because your loved one is gone, or are you going to celebrate because your loved one came this way?" I realized that I needed to celebrate the years I had with Aunt Eunice. As I thought about the fact that I had been blessed to have Aunt Eunice in my life, I started to feel better. Then I thought about one of my favorite quotes from noted author and poet Maya Angelou. Ms. Angelou said, "If you don't like something, change it. If you can't change it, change your attitude." I could not change the circumstances, so I decided to change my attitude, and it changed my thinking and my mood.

Reframe Your Thinking with an Attitude of Gratitude

Another powerful technique to beat the blues and over-come the spirit of depression is to think about the things in your life for which you are grateful. Take a moment and focus on the things that you have, rather than the things that you don't have. As my friend W. Mitchell said after he was para-lyzed in an airplane accident, "Before I was paralyzed, there were 10,000 things I could do. Now there are 9,000. I can either dwell on the 1,000 I've lost or focus on the 9,000 I have left."

Another technique to help you reframe your thinking to cultivate an attitude of gratitude is to add the words "at least" to the end of the sentence when you are talking about the chal-lenges that are trying to bring you down. For example: "My pay got cut, but at least I still have a job" or "I lost my job, but at least I still have my health!" Or, "I'm sick, but at least I'm still here!" When you add the phrase "at least" to the end of the sentence, you are changing your thinking. It allows you to focus on another perspective, a positive perspective, and from there you can start to reframe your thinking and overcome the grip of depression. When you have an attitude of gratitude, you see life from a different perspective. Every day is a holiday. Every meal is a feast, and every drink of water is a toast to the magnificent journey of life and love. Live your life with an atti-tude of gratitude!

Think about Helping Others

To think about helping others sounds so simplistic, but it is so incredibly impactful. Social scientists have found that changing your focus from yourself to helping others can be beneficial in overcoming depression. By looking at others and finding ways that you can help them, you can see that you are a valuable part of the culture and can become a helpful force of nature. Focusing your attention and energy on others can minimize your issues and help you realize how blessed you are. It's like the old saying, "I was feeling sorry for myself because I had no shoes until I met the person who had no feet." If you deflect your attention from your own problems and open your eyes to the situations and circumstances of those around you, you will find an opportunity to help others and, while doing so, help yourself!

I recommend you try to uplift others and encourage others, as it can have a tremendous impact on you. I feel that if you are willing to help others and spray a little perfume on them, you cannot help but get a little bit on you as well. Help others, and you will in turn truly help yourself!

Change Your Input

Another way to beat back depression and change your mood is to change your input! Your input determines your output. Rather than dwelling on the negative input that started you on the path to depression, I recommend you shift your attention away from the things that have sent you in the direction of depression and focus your attention elsewhere.

For me, music is a tremendous tool to help lift my spirits. In fact, I make it a habit to listen to uplifting music every day; no matter what is going on in my life, it always makes me feel better. At times, it pulls me out of a low point and helps me regain my equilibrium and return to a point of normalcy.

I'll never forget a time, some years ago, when I was in Annapolis, Maryland, to speak for a big hotel event. The event was during the evening, and I had arrived the night before to spend some time at the hotel and learn more about the employees' culture. After a tour in the morning, I had the afternoon off, and I went back to my room and turned on the television while I was getting ready to get some work done. The movie *Selena* was just beginning, and it captured my attention. I had heard about this beautiful young lady who became a superstar in the Hispanic community. It was an intriguing story, and because of the great music, I was drawn to it.

I sat and watched the whole film, and then at the end, this beautiful young lady was tragically killed by a deranged fan. I watched as her family mourned and the community grieved, and I was overtaken by an overwhelming sense of sadness. I was depressed! And then I realized that I had about an hour before I was to speak before a large group of people in the hotel ballroom. I knew I had to get over this depression and had to do it quickly, so I pulled out my iPod and put on "You've Got to Keep Kicking," a song written by my friend Tony Taylor that had been featured on one of my earlier albums. I listened to the song, and immediately the sadness dissipated and I started to feel better. As I listened to more of the songs in my "power play list," I got stronger and stronger, and in a short time I was back and ready to go out and fire up that audience!

In the Bible, it is noted that King Saul suffered from depression, and whenever that "distressing spirit" came upon him, he would call on David to come and play his harp to lift him out of his distress. It has been said that music can soothe the savage beast, even the savage beast that is within us!

Inspirational and uplifting music can brighten your day and give you hope; and when you have hope for the future, it can give you power in the present! The much-loved quotation is absolutely true: "Music hath charms to soothe a savage [beast], to soften rocks, or bend a knotted oak!"[1]

Fill Yourself with the Pure, the Powerful, and the Positive

Another way to reframe your thinking and beat depression is to fill yourself with the pure, the powerful, and the positive. Create a list of affirmations and quotations that align with your value system to lift your spirits. I often rely on scriptural references such as, "If God is for us, who can be against us?" (Romans 8:28-31) or "But those who wait on the Lord shall renew their strength; they shall mount up with wings as eagles; they shall run and not be weary, they shall walk and not faint" (Isaiah 40:31).

I recommend having a list of motivational and inspirational quotes or phrases that you can apply to challenging situations. Of course, my favorites are:

- A setback is nothing but a setup for a comeback!

- The best is yet to come!

- No matter what, I know that I am blessed and highly favored!

- When I am down to nothing, I know that God is up to something...and no matter what the situation, I and God make a majority!

I have learned that we must speak power into our lives, because our words have an impact on our thinking and our feeling! So I recommend you memorize scriptural and inspirational quotes to help you fight the drama of depression.

Rest and Rejuvenate

Another remedy for depression is a simple yet effective solution—rest and renew yourself. Sometimes, you need to get away and get some rest and rejuvenation so you can get back into the fight. I remember after one particularly trying day when I talked with my friend Greg Owen, an entrepreneur and success expert who lives in Sydney, Australia. Greg said, "Willie, this has been a tough fight, so I am going to go take an aspirin and a lie-down, and when I wake up I will be ready to fight again!"

Sometimes you just need to rest and renew yourself. We are all human, and we all get tired and need to rest to rejuvenate ourselves. Learn to get proper rest, exercise, and a proper diet, and it can have a profound impact on your battle with depression.

Some people have said that super success is the result of either inspiration or desperation, and I believe there is some truth in that statement. Sometimes we get our best ideas in extreme situations, when we are pressed to win and do not panic. There is a thin line between being pressed and being panicked, but it is a line that winners learn they cannot cross. Just as there is a thin line between confidence and arrogance, those who are successful learn where the line is and develop the discipline not to cross it.

Bob Johnson, the billionaire businessman who founded Black Entertainment Television, said, "The same hammer that shatters the glass, forges the steel!" We will all have challenges and difficulties in our lives, but we must develop ourselves so that we are able to not just go through those challenges, but grow through those challenges. Our response to life's challenges determines how the pressures of life affect us. These pressures can build us up and make us better—or break us down and make us bitter.

I recommend that you use the pressures of life to build you and make you into the diamond you were born to be! Don't just go through it, grow through it! Do not panic!

My good friend, speaker and author Dr. Terry Paulson, has a great book called *The Optimism Advantage: 50 Simple Truths to Transform Your Attitude and Actions into Results* (John Wiley & Sons, Inc., 2010). In the book, he does a tremendous job of helping use optimism to create massive success and wealth. He writes:

> Claiming the optimism advantage is not motivational hype. Optimism is an attitude that is earned through a track record of overcoming obstacles. The more setbacks and adversity you have handled, the more you come to believe that you can overcome the next one life gives you. Tough times can be the launching pad for great success. Optimists are realists who are problem solvers, not problem evaders. They want to know what obstacles they are facing so that they can get busy finding a solution. Optimists understand that wealth is really the intersection of income and impact. The more you see yourself solving problems, the more you go about the work and the more money becomes available to you. Make a point of making the commitment to turn your worry into constructive action every day. Take it one day at a time, just take it and make it happen. Every successful

entrepreneur will tell you that the journey to wealth is filled with closed doors, setbacks, failures, and the satisfying joy of achieving success along the way. Don't let anyone call you a victim; you are a resilient survivor who is choosing to live your dream. Wealth is not the only goal; in reality it is the byproduct of transforming our gifts into a mission that makes a difference people are willing to pay for. When you find your gifts, identify your mission, and claim a positive attitude, wealth and meaning are on the way!

ENDNOTE

1. The original quote was written by William Congreve in *The Mourning Bride:* "Music hath charms to soothe the savage breast, to soften rocks, or bend a knotted oak." Often misquoted and widely known as "savage beast."

DON'T WILLINGLY PARTICIPATE OR COMMISERATE

I like to say, "Too many people follow the crowd, even if the crowd is going in the wrong direction." That being said, I encourage you to decide that you will not participate willingly in commiserating, and the definitive word in this statement is "willingly."

For many years when I spoke about economic downturns, I would quickly say, "I am not participating in this recession!" I was fine with that until I realized that everyone feels the impact of tough economic times. Also, I realized that telling someone who just lost his or her home or retirement savings to "not participate" was somewhat disingenuous. It was not meant to be disingenuous, but nevertheless, it was hard to tell someone who was living a terrible financial nightmare to just ignore what was going on in his or her life. In my heart, I wanted to tell people, "Do not buy into the doom and gloom and the bad news and negative thinking!" But you cannot avoid the impact of some events in life, no matter how hard you try.

I had to think about my message and come up with a statement that was clearer, one that conveyed strength and a caring message for those who had been involuntarily sucked into an economic mess. As I thought about it, I realized that we cannot choose to be pulled into economic downturns, but we can choose not to participate willingly! In other words, we do not have to get in line and go along with the program. We need not contribute to the problem, but rather we should be part of the solution.

When we willingly participate, we become volunteer victims. Volunteer victims are people who voluntarily position themselves for victimhood. I was watching *The Apprentice* television show with Donald Trump, and he had a similar take on getting in line with those who are willing to lose. A contestant was part of the team that lost, but she did not contribute to the team losing. Yet to be supportive of the team leader, she volunteered to go back in the boardroom with the team leader, even though she was not one of the culprits who caused the loss. When Mr. Trump asked why she was back in the boardroom, he was told she volunteered. He immediately fired her! He said, "Never voluntarily get in the line for execution! Don't even get close to the area if you do not have to!" It was a tough lesson, but it was true. Far too many people get in line for execution with tough economies when they need not do so. Do not get in line with all the people who have decided to buy into the gloom and doom of the times. Do not be like sheep who are lining up to go to slaughter!

I believe that being a willing participant is like walking around with a *kick me* sign taped to your back. Life will kick you, and keep kicking you if you allow it to do so. I often say that life looks for people it can knock down and keep down; those who are defiant are those who make life leave them alone. If you are willing to fight back and be defiant, life will typically leave you alone and go look for a wimp to keep down.

I travel a lot, and on one trip I got to the airport and needed to quickly check my luggage and get to my flight. It was a cold winter day, so I immediately went to the inside check-in area to check my luggage, but the line was super long. I knew that because of the long line I would not be able to catch my flight; I needed to look for other options. I buttoned up my coat and went outside, because there is usually a curbside check-in option. It was cold, but there was a much shorter line. I quickly checked my luggage and was off to catch my flight.

As I walked past the line inside, there was a young lady who was anxiously looking at her watch with a pained look on her face. I stopped and asked her if everything was okay. She said she had been in the line for a long time and needed to check her luggage. I asked her why she was in the line when there were other options, and she responded, "Because every-one else was in the line!" I called the skycap who had just helped me and asked him if he would help her. He looked at her ticket and said, "Too late! That flight has already closed!" Turns out she missed her flight because she got in line with all the other folks, thinking there were no other options.

In life, don't get in line with the other people—check out the options. Jesus taught, "And if the blind leads the blind, both will fall into a ditch" (Matthew 15:14). I encourage people to look at the options and make the decision that works best for them.

Take the *kick me* sign off your back, and make up your mind that you will not participate *willingly* in economic downturns, recessions, depressions, or anything else. You might feel it, but you need not be a willing party to it. Too many people follow the crowd, even if the crowd is going in the wrong direction.

We do not have to go along with the status quo without at least giving a fight. There is a statement on my wall in my office that states, "Life is a fight for territory. When you stop fighting for what you want, what you don't want automatically takes over!" It is in these moments of challenge that we will either move forward toward our goals and dreams or we will fall back toward our fears. The choice literally is up to you!

It is in these moments that we must look at encouraging ourselves to get off the canvas of life and get back in the fight. It is wonderful if you have a team of people cheering you on, but sometimes you have no one to help you get up but yourself. That is why it is critical to learn to have positive conversations with yourself. We can make up our minds that we will go kicking and screaming, and will not stop fighting. Do not go down without a fight!

In other words, I am telling you that it is important that you be unreasonable and defiant! That's right, be unreasonable and be defiant! You must be willing to fight for your goals. Think about people who say they want to reach their goals, yet they act like they will do it only if it's easy. That is how most people act about their goals; they will work toward their goal only if it is not an inconvenience. No! That is not the way to achieve your goal. You must want it and must be willing to fight to make it a reality.

I have said for years that you must be unreasonable to get what you want in life. To be unreasonable does not mean being rude or nasty, but rather that you will not take no for an answer. You will not give up on your dreams and goals just because others cannot see your vision. If it is not other people, it will be the circumstances of life that will suggest that you should just accept the status quo, the way things are. I say you must be willing to be unreasonable. Life will say, "Just be reasonable and accept this situation," but I reply with, *"No,* that is not acceptable, and I cannot accept that option." Again, you need not be rude or nasty to take a stand. You simply need to make up your mind that you will not willingly participate. To beat a recession or economic downturn, you must be willing to fight, fight for your dreams and goals, and keep fighting.

The Bible says that we are to have life and have it more abundantly, not less abundantly. The recession, the depression, and all the other economic calamities are not the way God wants us to live. They are demonic situations, and they need to go right back where they came from...from hell. That is why I wake up every morning and give God thanks for another day and another opportunity to live my dreams, not my fears. That is why I give God glory every day for life and the opportunity to make a difference and make a profit. That is why I wake up every day and say, "Good morning, Lord!" rather than, "Oh Lord, it's morning!" That is why I say, every day, "This is going to be a great day, because I have life and I can choose to make it a great day!" I cannot choose what happens to me, and I cannot choose what happens around me, but I have complete choice about what happens in me...and I choose to be happy, grateful, and excited about this upcoming day!

Do not get in line with all the people who have decided to buy into the gloom and doom of the times. Make up your mind that you will not willingly participate, because otherwise you will be sucked in by all the bad news and gloom and doom that are a part of the media spin. That media spin will not only influence you but can have an impact on you for years to come.

I saw an old friend with whom I'd grown up, and I asked about his brother, who was my elementary school playmate. My friend asked if I would call his brother, because his brother had been going through some tough times and needed some encouragement to get back up on his feet. I said I would be happy to do so, and made the call. After a few initial greetings with my friend, I said, "So I saw your brother, and he asked me to call. How are things going?" My friend responded, "Things are not going too well. I have been out of work for a long time, and I am way behind on my bills." I then asked, "Where have you been looking for work?" He responded, "Well, I haven't been looking." I said, "Why not?" His response amazed me. He said, "I haven't been looking because the people on television say there are no jobs!" Unfortunately, many people buy into this thinking, because they trust the news media as the truth tellers of society, when really they are sharing a perspective, *their* perspective of the truth.

Yes, it is true that in tough times it is harder to get a job, yet it is not impossible to get a job. How do I know? Well, while people in the United States are talking about not being able to get a job, people who come here from other countries often get not only one job but multiple jobs! These jobs might not be the top of the line, but they are ways to keep the bills paid until they can get a top-of-the-line job. When people say, "There are no jobs," I always wonder...*If there are no jobs, why is there still a need for newspaper employment advertisements? There are still pages and pages of jobs being advertised every day.*

My former classmate had bought into the gloom and the doom! He had become a willing participant in the bad times. Network marketing expert Hope Elliott said to me when I came to speak for her group, "POOR is Passing Over Opportunities Regularly!" Open your mind to possibilities and do not buy into the gloom and doom. Remember, sometimes opportunities will knock on the door and we will say, "Stop making all that noise, go away!" Open your eyes and your mind to the great opportunities that are all around you!

The secret to succeeding is a willingness to think beyond the gloom and doom and look for opportunities. You must not become a willing participant in the economic downturn. You must fight back and keep fighting back!

DON'T COMMISERATE

The word *commiserate* is a word we usually think of when people sit around and bemoan the loss of their favorite sports team, but when striving for success in the face of setbacks, the word has impact. I want to warn you against commiserating in the game of life. The practice of going around talking about how bad things are to people in your network will get you nowhere. Often, when bad things happen in life, we find people who make a habit of going around talking about the bad things—and that is all they do. It not only adds fuel to a fire that is already raging, but it also creates a doom and gloom scenario and a victim mentality.

People who commiserate are the ones who call and say, "Did you hear the bad news about Company X going out of business?" or, "Did you hear about Company Y laying off more people?" Woe is me, woe is me.

People who commiserate are the people who would rather complain about problems than to do anything to fix them. We have a choice. We can talk about the all the bad news and keep repeating it, or we can go about making a difference. We can complain about the dark or we can light a candle and be a light in a dark world.

It is like the story of the old farmer who was sitting on his porch with his old hound dog. The dog was just sitting there howling. A stranger came by and asked the old farmer why the dog was howling and making so much noise, and the old farmer replied, "Because he is sitting on a nail."

The stranger asked, "Why doesn't he get up?"

The old farmer responded, "Because it doesn't hurt badly enough!"

Many people will get in the line and complain about the situation but will not do much to change the circumstances. You must decide to stay away from the negative talkers who do nothing but talk. Talking about problems without offering solutions creates a lose/lose scenario. It is important that you do not allow yourself to get into the trap of complaining about a situation in your life without offering a solution to the problem.

Commiserating adds fuel to a fire that can have an impact on your psyche and your emotional stability. A constant barrage of negative information can lead to a negative view of the world.

To commiserate can create a psychological construct, a self-fulfilling prophecy—a situation that is not yet true but has the potential to become true, because you have created an expectation that it will become reality. The more you talk about bad news, the deeper its impact will be on your psyche and your physiology, and the more your mind moves to make it a reality. Scripture says, "For as he thinks in his heart, so is he" (Proverbs 23:7).

A study was done at the University of Texas regarding the impact of bad news on the psyche and physiology of athletes. A football player was selected to be one of the case studies. After practice, he was asked by a researcher, "How are you doing?" He responded, "Outstanding! Fired up! It was a great practice and I'm ready to take on the world!" The person in the study responded by saying, "Are you sure? You look a little sick!" The football player replied, "No, I feel great!"

A short while later the football player was approached by a different person associated with the study and asked the same question. The football player responded, "I feel fine." The person in the study said, "All right, but you look a little sick." Over the next few hours, different people stopped the football player and asked the same set of questions and gave the same "you look sick" response. By the end of the day, the football player was feeling sick and depressed, because he had been inundated with so much gloom and doom and bad news about his health. In reality, he was not sick, but the high level of negative news made him think he was. Dear reader, it is critical that you stay away from the gloom-and-doomers and the negative provocateurs!

I met a gentleman one day who had seen me on television. He came up to me and started rattling off about how bad things were for his business and business in general. He said, "Did you hear about how bad things are here and how bad things are there? Did you hear that so-and-so lost their business? Did you hear?" Before he could get a full head of steam, I stopped him and said, "If you are looking for someone to commiserate with, you've got the wrong guy. I am aware that there are some tough situations all around, but I decided I am not going to dwell on the problems. Instead, I am thinking and looking at all the great opportunities. Now is the time when the winners are made! I am working hard and I am planning to have my best year yet. I realize there are some challenges out in the business world; but wherever there are challenges, there are opportunities. I am planning to work hard and find those opportunities, and I cannot find any opportunities if I continue to look at the situation as hopeless. I will be like Hannibal, the great African military man, who said, 'If you cannot find a way, make a way!' Hannibal could find no way to defeat the Romans with a frontal attack, so he did the unthinkable. He used African elephants to transport his troops over the Alps and attacked the Romans from the rear, and he defeated them— because when there was no opportunity he decided to create an opportunity. Now is the time to create some great new opportunities."

I realized that part of the reason this man's business was suffering was because he was dwelling on the negatives about business, rather than the positives. If you focus on the negative points in your life, those are what will grow, but the same is true for the positive. Be aware of the negative issues, but focus on the positive, the possibilities. Whatever you focus on and think about is what you will become and what you will grow.

Make a point that you will not sign up, line up, or whine up about the recessions of life; rather, you will stand up and fight for your dreams and goals, and never ever give up on your future and all the incredible possibilities that lie within you.

DON'T LET YOUR PRIDE POISON YOUR PROSPERITY

If you are going to turn your setbacks into greenbacks, it is necessary to get past your pride and make the decision that you will not let your pride poison your prosperity. Pride is an interesting word, because we all are expected to have self-respect and pride in ourselves, but too much pride can keep us from achieving our goals and dreams. Pride can create conceit and an unwillingness to try new ideas. I want to concentrate on this point. We all have pride and some level of self-esteem, but we also need to be aware that pride left unchecked can alter your view of the world and your perspective on taking advantage of the opportunities that will help you grow your success.

To turn a setback into a financial comeback will take some new thinking and some new actions, because it is true that if you keep doing what you have been doing, you will keep getting what you have been getting. You have to do some different things, and do some things differently.

Often, what stops people from success is not their ability but their pride. They are overly concerned about what "people" will say rather than what their heart says. It is best to ask yourself these questions: *Did I give my best? Did I give my all? Did I have integrity and character? Did I hold up my end of the bargain with God? (Because God is going to do His part!) Did I remember that God's gift to me is life...my gift to God is what I do with my life!* As Martin Luther King Jr. so aptly said, "If a man is called to be a street sweeper, he should sweep streets as Michelangelo painted, and Shakespeare wrote poetry! He should sweep streets so well that all the hosts of heaven and earth will proclaim, 'there lived a great street sweeper who did his job well!'" To that I say, you must not let pride stand in the way of your wealth! You must not let your pride poison your prosperity.

Far too often I see people who are struggling financially but not doing anything to turn their finances around because they are trying to put up a façade of success. As my friend Larry Winget, the host of the television show *Big Spender,* says, "There are a lot of people who could turn their lives around, but they have too much pride, and therefore they are too stupid to become wealthy. They are putting on an act that they are doing well, when they can hardly pay their basic bills. They are $30,000 millionaires! Big hat, no cattle!"

You cannot let your pride get in the way of your wealth building. Some people feel that some work is beneath them. They feel that it would bring a stigma to them if people know they were doing supposedly "demeaning" work, yet they are struggling to pay their bills. I believe any work that is moral and legal is honorable.

WORKING THROUGH A DOWNTURN

My friend Duke Greene is a great example of how to build wealth and not get stuck on minor issues, but rather always keep your focus on the major issues. Duke Greene was a guest on my SiriusXM Radio show and shared a story that had the phones ringing off the hook. He told how he started the company IBS (International Business Services) in the 1970s, built it into a national powerhouse, and then sold it in the 1990s. The company was worth $96 million, and he had offices all across the country with thousands of employees.

However, during an economic downturn in the 1970s, he made up his mind that he did not want to lose any of the great people he had hired, so he decided not to lay off any of his people. As the CEO, he was the highest paid person on the payroll, so he took his salary and contributed it to help pay the employees. After a few months of living on his savings, he realized he needed to do something to pay his personal bills. He knew that the economic downturn was a temporary situation and that the economy would come back, so he just needed to get through the tough months. So he worked all day as the CEO of IBS, and at night he drove a truck, like he had done in college, to make ends meet. He said that leaders do not let the circumstances stop them from doing what is necessary to grow their businesses. As long as it is moral and legal, it is good business and honorable work.

Someone called in to ask a question after Duke shared his story. The person asked, "What if you have been a professional and now you have to do something that is beneath you?" Duke responded, "You have to get over it! You have to realize that this is temporary! It is not forever, it is just something you have to do to pay your bills and get through the tough times!"

I know that economic downturns and slow times in business can be overwhelming, but if you do not panic, but instead look for opportunities, you will see that they are all around you. If you can get past what people will think about you on the front end, you will find that they will have great respect for you on the back end!

FROM THE GROUND UP

Years ago I was invited to speak at the Wendy's Restaurant Youth Leadership Conference in Fort Lauderdale, Florida. The conference was created by the founder of Wendy's, Dave Thomas. Dave was retired and serving as the Chairman of the Board of Wendy's at the time, and he was spending his time helping develop young people into leaders. When his office called and asked if I would be the keynote speaker for their conference, I was thrilled and gladly accepted. As a part of the weekend we were told that Dave Thomas would like to have us over for dinner the night before the conference. So my wife and I flew to Fort Lauderdale the day before the conference and had dinner with Dave Thomas at his waterside mansion.

During dinner I asked Dave how he started Wendy's. His answer is an incredible testament to the power of not letting pride poison your prosperity. Dave told me that he was adopted, and during his teen years he got a job at a local restaurant. He said he loved the restaurant business and as a result he dropped out of school so he could work more hours. His friends laughed at him and told him it was embarrassing to work at the restaurant, scrubbing floors and flipping burgers.

In fact they laughed at him and called him "Hamburger Boy!" But Dave didn't care. He made up his mind that he was not going to let what others thought of him be the thing that determined his destiny.

During his time at the restaurant, Dave met an older gentleman named Harland Sanders, who had started a restaurant chain called Kentucky Fried Chicken. Dave ended up taking over some of the struggling Kentucky Fried Chicken restaurants in the Ohio area and turned them around. He sold those restaurants and then decided to start a hamburger restaurant with custom-made hamburgers. He named the restaurant after his daughter, Wendy—and the rest is history! Dave went on to become one of the most successful businessmen in American history and the most successful founder-turned-television spokesman ever.

Dave Thomas did not let his pride poison his prosperity. He was a high school dropout who never stopped thinking about his goals and dreams and was willing to work hard to make his dreams become realities. He was proud of going back to school and passed his General Educational Development (GED) tests, but he was most noted for his hard work and his MBA, which is what he called his "Mop and Bucket Attitude." No job was beneath him, and all work was honorable, as long as it didn't offend the laws of God and the laws of the land.

And by the way, many of those people who laughed at him and called him "Hamburger Boy" ended up calling him "Boss!" He was able to make those who laughed at him on the front end eat their words and work for him on the back end. Do not be concerned about what others think of you; focus on your dreams and goals!

TAKE OUT THE TRASH

Another example of someone who did not let his pride poison his prosperity is Wayne Huizenga. Wayne Huizenga made his wealth as a trash man. He was born during the Great Depression and grew up poor. As a young man he started working for a family who had a trash company. After a couple of years, he had saved enough money to buy his own trash truck, and he started his own company. Many laughed at him because he was a trash man, but he never let his pride get in the way of his prosperity. He would pick up trash from 2:00 A.M. until midday, and for the rest of the day he would go door to door to drum up business. He bought more trash trucks, hired more people, and eventually bought his biggest competitor. Eventually, Huizinga's company, Waste Management, Inc., went public. He continued to grow the business; and in time he became wealthy and even bought the Miami Dolphins football team and the Florida Marlins baseball team. He went from hauling trash to hauling dollars to the bank, because he refused to let others determine his possibilities. He refused to let his pride poison his prosperity.

Let me say this emphatically: You must not let what other people think about you stop you from taking action. You must take action. Often we get stymied and end up doing nothing because of our pride. We can get overwhelmed by fear or low expectations, but these can create a lack of activity and therefore a lack of success. It is critical that you make up your mind, get going, and take some action.

So what should we do? Something, anything...just move forward! You can't sit there waiting for success to come to you. If you fail, then try again, start over and keep trying, just do something positive toward your goal. Don't wait or it just may be too late! Take action! And remember—massive success is always the best revenge!

DON'T STOP THINKING AND DREAMING ABOUT THE POWER AND POSSIBILITIES OF TOMORROW

"The future belongs to those who believe in the beauty of their dreams."
—ELEANOR ROOSEVELT

The race does not always go to the swift or to the strong, but to the one who endures until the end.

The next step to turn your setbacks into greenbacks is "Don't stop thinking about tomorrow." This concept is taken from the Fleetwood Mac song, which has become one of the top songs on my iTunes favorite play list. I had heard the song years ago, but never really listened to the lyrics; when I took time to really listen to the lyrics, I realized it was my kind of song, something that would uplift and inspire people to live better!

If you listen to the song, you will find that it implores us to keep going and keep thinking about the future, because those who keep working on their goals typically create better futures. When things are tough and we are feeling low, we need to look up and think up, so that we can see things differently and recognize new possibilities. Don't stop, don't give up on your dreams and goals; instead, keep thinking about tomorrow and the better days to come. The chorus of the song implores us to have a positive outlook, positive in-look, and positive up-look!

Step 4 has multiple meanings that can best be demonstrated by the emphasis communication technique. In this technique, the way you emphasize the different words in the statement—*Don't. Stop. Thinking. About. Tomorrow.*—can alter the meaning of the statement.

A few years ago, my wife and I started teaching a class on communications skills at our church, and we used a resource called Speaking with Bold Assurance, developed by Bert Decker. Bert is a friend and one of the top media coaches in the country. In this program, he taught about the power of emphasis, and how in communications the word you choose to emphasize can have a tremendous impact on the meaning of the statement. As an example, Bert uses the phrase "I. Didn't. Say. You. Stole. That. Car." I want you to repeat this statement out loud seven times, and each time, I want you to put the emphasis on a different word. First, I want you to emphasize the word *I* in the statement; the next time, emphasize the word *didn't*. The third time, emphasize the word *say*, and so on. You will see that the meaning of the statement drastically changes depending on where you place the emphasis.

If we follow the same process for the statement "Don't stop thinking about tomorrow," we will see that the messages that are generated are all different. Yet they all apply in helping you turn your economic setbacks into greenbacks!

First is the word *don't*. *Don't* stop thinking about tomorrow! To turn your setbacks into greenbacks, it is critical for you to be dogmatic in your thinking about coming back. You must not even consider that you will not be able to get through this tough stretch. Don't even think about it! Don't let the negative thoughts get in your mind. Oh they might try to invade your thoughts—but you, ultimately, control your thinking. Norman Vincent Peale, author of the landmark book, *The Power of Positive Thinking,* said, "You may not be able to keep birds from flying above your head, but you don't have to let them build a nest in your hair." Negative thoughts will fly all around your mind, but don't even consider that you will not be able to survive this economic situation. You must stay positive, and if you have to talk to yourself and encourage yourself, so be it! Get a *don't* mindset, and by the pure nature of the word, you will become more willing to keep fighting.

By placing the emphasis on the word *stop,* the focus shifts to the fact that you must keep hitting the rock, keep pushing, and keep trying to achieve your goals. As you keep hitting the rock, you know that if you hit it long enough and hard enough it will eventually break! Once the rock, the hard obstacle in front of you, breaks, you will not know for sure whether it broke because the hundredth hit was so powerful that it shattered the rock, or the rock was worn down from the constant and consistent battering and finally broke due to the cumulative impact of all the hits. Whatever way you think, you must make the commitment that you will not stop, that you will not give up, that you will not give in. "Don't *stop!*" The main thing is that the rock, the obstacle in your way, finally broke down and is no longer in your way! Don't *stop!*

Next is *thinking*. Keep thinking up new ideas and new ways to turn this setback into a comeback. I believe that most times when you have a problem, it is usually not a money problem but rather an idea problem. It is time to come up with some new ideas and new thinking. Albert Einstein said that the thinking that got you this far will not get you to the next level. So we must be willing to think up! We need to think bigger, bolder, and better! We must continue to push the envelope and come up with new ideas and new strategies. If one idea doesn't work, come up with another idea. Keep thinking about the future and all the incredible opportunities that are within our grasp. Don't stop *thinking* about tomorrow.

The next word that we will emphasize is the word *about*. When we emphasize this word, we come to the realization that there are tremendous opportunities all about, all around us! Is it a tough market? Yes! Is it a tough economic landscape? Yes! Is it going to be hard? Yes! But the truth be told, business is challenging even in good times; it is just more challenging now. So this is the time when we develop the muscle that will fuel the fire when we get back to a good economy.

Another part of thinking *about* the possibilities is to remember the last time we were in a tough economic situation. What did we do then? Remember what we did to get through that experience, and just do it again, but do more of it! Think back and remind yourself of past successes and past experiences. I often think about my first summer as a speaker. I was brand-new, didn't know anyone, and didn't know much about the speaking business. I had been speaking at schools during the school year, but when the school year ended in June, I didn't have any work and therefore didn't have any money. I was definitely in an economic downturn. I didn't know how I was going to pay my mortgage or my bills, so I got on the phone and literally went through the *Yellow Pages* asking people if they had a need for a speaker.

I finally got two small contracts—one to speak for a youth arts camp and the other to be a part-time speaker/counselor for a small community-based youth theatrical group. Somehow I made it through the summer and paid my bills. Once school started again I got calls from some of the administrators who had worked with the two programs during the summer; they booked me in their individual schools and helped me get bookings at their brother and sister schools. I made it through. Over the years, whenever I have had times that were tight financially, I think about that summer and how I got through those times by faith, focus, and follow-through. Because I made it through that time, I can sleep at night now, because I remember that when I didn't know anyone and didn't know much about speaking, I refused to quit—I made it then and I will make it now! Remind yourself about the successes of the past and use them to empower you as you go forward into the future.

The last part of this phrase is the word *tomorrow.* In the hit movie and Broadway play *Annie,* the star of the show, an orphan girl named Annie, sings a song called "Tomorrow." In the song, she proclaims that the sun will come up tomorrow—that you can depend on the fact that tomorrow, there will be sun. And if you think about those bright tomorrows, it will take away all the tears, the pain, and the sorrow. The tears of today will be replaced by the smiles of tomorrow.

DON'T GIVE UP

"Don't quit! Keep looking up!
Because if you can look up, you can get up!"
—LES BROWN

This advice to not give up sounds elementary and simple, but for some reason when tough times come around, people seem to forget that they must not give up. This is an absolute necessity for turning your situation around and turning your setbacks into greenbacks. You simply cannot give up!

You would think this would be something that we could not forget, because every motivational book I have ever read has had some information about the power of perseverance and persistence. In tough times, though, we seem to forget this important ingredient in the success formula.

Why do people forget such an important ingredient? Sometimes people forget because the massive amount of bad news that floods the marketplace overwhelms them. Sometimes they forget because they have taken their eyes off their dreams and goals and started to focus on their problems. As I learned years ago, when you take your eyes off your possibilities and look at your problems and circumstances, you start to suffer.

There is a great example of this in the Bible. Jesus was walking on the water, and Peter stepped out of the boat and walked on the water toward Jesus. Peter was fine as long as he kept his eyes on Jesus, but as soon as he looked down and saw the water, he started to sink.

A more recent example is Bob Wieland, the legless marathon runner. Bob was an all-star athlete well on his way to becoming a professional baseball player when he was drafted to serve in Vietnam. While in battle, one of his comrades was hit and Bob went to rescue him. While trying to bring his friend to safety, Bob was hit with a mortar round and lost both of his legs. Rather than dwelling on his lost baseball career or on losing his ability to walk and run, Bob Wieland chose to focus on the challenges that were ahead. He decided to take on the challenge of running a marathon—26 miles—without legs. He would go the 26 miles by placing his hands on the ground and swinging his body forward. Each "step" involved swinging his body with his hands. When he ran his first marathon, it took many days. By the time he finished, his hands were raw and bloodied. The pain was intense, yet when a newspaper reporter asked him how he handled the intense pain he responded that the only time he felt it was when he took his eyes off the goal!

When you focus on your problems, you will find that life becomes much more challenging and difficult. A wide array of positive possibilities are available all around you, but you must decide whether to focus on your problems or your possibilities. Those who focus on their problems without thinking about solutions or coming up with positive possibilities are those destined to just survive, not thrive, in the midst of the tough times.

Instead, focus on the fact that you have life, and live in a time and place where success is not only possible but actually can be achieved. How do I know this is true? I know because history has taught that some of the greatest businesses were born in the midst of tough times. IBM, Hewlett-Packard,

Microsoft, Disney, and Walmart are all examples of this. And some of the wealthiest people in the world started building their wealth in the midst of tough economic times.

Those who win over the long term are those who decided to focus on the good news rather than the bad news. (That is one of the reasons I recently started a new organization called Jolley Good News to help people get positive news, rather than a constant diet of negative news. Visit www.jolleygoodnews. org for more information on this organization and how it can help you to grow and succeed at the next level.)

I believe you must make a commitment to fill yourself with the pure, the powerful, and the positive. I believe that we should have a reservoir from which to draw inspiration and motivation. I believe that we should dig our wells before we are thirsty and start reading and listening to positive information before we need it. During tough times, people seem to forget the basics and resort to the old ways of focusing on the bad news that comes from the news media. The news media consistently make a habit of looking at life through a negative lens. If the sun is halfway shining, they will say "partly cloudy" rather than "partly sunny!" The old idiom for the news: "If it bleeds, it leads!"

Sometimes people forget the basic principle of not giving up because they have been influenced by their negative, small-minded friends and family members. If you are going to turn your setbacks into greenbacks, it is critical that you surround yourself with positive people. I often talk about *dream-busters*—those who lurk around and make it their job to kill dreams. Unfortunately, these are often people in our inner circles. They are people we love, who actually love us; they are not trying to be mean-spirited when they crush your hopes and dreams and tell you they are just trying to be real! They just happen to suffer from *possibility blindness*. They say they are trying to be real, and figure that because times are tough you should just lie down and die—all while the winners are pushing forward and seeing opportunity and possibility.

The dreams of tomorrow can focus our actions today. Dr. Stephen Covey, author of the landmark best-selling book *The 7 Habits of Highly Effective People,* said, "The most effective people always start with the end in mind, then they move towards that picture!" To turn your setbacks into greenbacks, you must keep thinking about the future and how things can get better.

The following is a song on my "Money Making Music and Motivation" CD that speaks about the power of being motivated, highly motivated.

Highly Motivated

(written by Willie Jolley and Paul Minor)

Motivated, highly motivated, motivated
gonna take it to the top.
Motivated, highly motivated, motivated,
I'm never gonna stop.

I had a job, a job I really hated
It made me sick, but it got me motivated.
I knew this was not where I was meant to be
I didn't want to stay but I was too afraid to leave.

But then one day I got my check and
there was almost nothing there.
I went to the boss; he laughed and said he didn't care.
My kids were at home hungry; I was about to lose my home
That's when I decided I had to make it on my own.

Motivated, highly motivated, motivated
gonna take it to the top.
Motivated, highly motivated, motivated,
I'm never gonna stop.

My friends said I was crazy when I told them all goodbye
But the only one who's crazy is the one who's afraid to try.
They said I wouldn't make it, said I would not survive
But I knew I had to make it, it was either do or die.

So I grabbed hold of my dream and I put it in my heart
I stepped out on my faith and learned to really trust in God.
I knew I had to fight, fight with all my power
Then things started happening, blessings
came, oh hour after hour.

Motivated, highly motivated, motivated
gonna take it to the top.
Motivated, highly motivated, motivated,
I'm never gonna stop.

I found that dreams do come true, if you believe,
Believe in you.
Don't worry about what others say,
If you're serious you'll make a way.

Hannibal said, "If you cannot find
a way, then make a way!"
See it doesn't matter so much what
happens around you, or to you
What matters is what happens in you!

When people stomp on your dreams
Don't get mad! Don't get even!
Get ahead! Because massive success, is the best revenge!

So when people laugh at you and they try to put you down,
Take that negative and turn it all around!

Grab hold of your dream; let it set your soul on fire.
Activate your faith and take it higher, higher!

Yeah, going to take it to the top!
I'm never going to stop.
If you've got faith, God's got the power
To bless your life, hour after hour.

Keep the faith, keep the desire
Keep reaching up, until you reach the sky!
Never going to stop believing what I can do.

I've got the power, you can have it too.
Start with the dream, add the desire.
Turn on your faith, and take it higher.
Take it to the top! Yeah!

Someone said in life, "You've got to
pray, like it all depends on God
And work like it all depends on you!"
Folks, it's time to get motivated...highly motivated!
It's time to live your dreams!

As I thought about the steps I had used to turn my economic setback into a comeback, I realized that one of the first steps is to make the commitment to never stop trying. This is a concept that is as old as time. In every success manual I have ever read (and there are thousands), I have seen the statement that you must persist and persevere. Yet as I learned more about success, I realized that persistence and perseverance are actually quite different.

To *persist* means to keep going after your goal in an obstinate, repetitive way. To keep hitting, keep fighting and keep working on your goal until you achieve it. Thomas Edison was persistent; he failed more than a thousand times in his quest to invent a light bulb, yet he refused to give up, and ultimately achieved his goal. I like to say that "persistence breaks down resistance!"

To *persevere* is to cultivate the attitude that somehow, some way, you will get through the tough times and get to a better place in your life. You will be the last person standing. I like the cartoon of the little frog that is holding on to a rope that has a knot in it; the caption reads, "When you get to the end of your rope, tie a knot and hold on!"

It is important that you persist and persevere in tough times to achieve your goals and turn your economic setbacks into greenbacks. It is common to implore people to persist and persevere, but it is uncommon to see people actually taking this advice to heart and doing it. Statistics show that most people do not achieve their goals and dreams because they simply give up. And I have seen many people give up when they are within striking distance of their goal. I have a family member who worked hard to develop a team for her network marketing company; when she got her first check, it was less than she had expected and she got angry and quit, not realizing that all rivers start with a drip of water. I can remember when I started writing books. Initially I was making just a few pennies per book; yet as more people started talking about the books and telling their friends, my pennies turned into dimes, then quarters, then dollars, all because I did not stop! Don't stop! Don't quit! Don't give up!

BELIEVE IN THE POWER
OF YOUR DREAMS

Dreams are the seeds for success. You have to have a dream. Every single success story I have ever read or heard about talks about the power of dreams. Scripture says that "Where there is no vision, the people perish" (Proverbs 29:18 KJV). Yet what goes unsaid is that *with* a vision people will flourish! You must have a vision! You must have a dream, a goal of what is possible in the future—and not dwell only on what is going on today. Dreams and goals give us hope for the future and give us hope for the present. We all know about the power of dreams and goals for helping us focus and get a game plan; yet I want to say that we need dreams and goals in tough times as well, because they give us hope and fuel for climbing out of the valley and up the rough side of the mountain.

There is power in our dreams; we should hold fast to them and let them empower us to achieve. An exciting movie called *The Opus* (www.theopusmovie.com) is making its way around the world. It is a follow-up to the hit movie *The Secret*, but with a different perspective. *The Opus* talks about the fact that success is the result of a process. The process involves vision (the power of a dream), planning (the power of preparation), and performance (the power of taking action and making the dream into a reality). Like *The Secret*, *The Opus* features selected experts who give teaching points throughout the movie, yet it also has a Disney-like story interwoven through the messages from the experts. I was honored to be asked to be one of the experts, and in one of my messages, I share my favorite story about the power of dreams.

It was a hot summer day in the summer of 1944, on the campus of Morehouse College in Atlanta, Georgia. The esteemed president of the college, Dr. Benjamin Mays, was sitting in his office; he was a dignified man with gray hair, wearing a suit and dabbing perspiration from his brow.

There was a knock on the door. Dr. Mays said, "Come in," and the door swung open to show a man and a teenage boy. Dr. Mays jumped to his feet and moved quickly to grab the hand of the man, his old friend, Reverend Martin Luther King Sr.—Daddy King.

"Come in, my friend!" Dr. Mays proclaimed.

Daddy King stepped in and said, "Dr. Mays, I know you are busy, so I won't take a lot of your time. I just came by to introduce you to my son Marty. Marty is 15 years old and just graduated from high school. He is going to college here in the fall and I need a big favor." Daddy King continued, "I don't need help with tuition or room and board; what I need is bigger! This boy has something special inside of him, I can just sense it, and I want to ask if you would teach him how to dream! Would you teach my son how to dream big dreams?"

Dr. Mays handed young Marty a piece of paper and told him to read it daily. On the paper Dr. Mays had written:

> It must be borne in mind that the tragedy of life does not lie in not reaching your goal. The tragedy lies in not having a goal to reach for! It is not a calamity to die with your dreams unfulfilled, but it is a calamity not to dream. It is not a disaster to be unable to capture your ideal, but it is a disaster to have no ideals to capture. It is not a disgrace not to reach the stars, but it is a disgrace to have no stars to reach for. Not failure, but low aim is sin!

I implore you to dream big dreams! I love the quote of a father who said to his son, "Dream dreams that are so big that you cannot achieve them in one lifetime."

What are your goals? What are your dreams? Everything you use today started in someone's mind. It started as a thought and went on to become a manifestation of that thought. Success always starts on the inside and then manifests itself on the outside. As Dr. Dennis Kimbro, author of *What Makes the Great Great,* shared on my radio show, "First is the thought, then comes the thing. First is the inner, which creates the outer." If the dream is big enough, the problems don't matter.

HOW TO SET GOALS THAT GET YOU GOING

Scripture says, write the vision, make it plain, that he who reads it may run the race! You need to have written dreams and goals and read them regularly to keep you focused on where you want to go and what you want to achieve. The reason I don't make New Year's resolutions is that they typically are not written and are usually forgotten by the end of January. Yet goals that are written give you power! If you want to create wealth, it is important that you write down your dreams and goals and read them regularly.

One additional step to creating wealth is to determine *why* you want to hit your goals. First you need a goal, but if you are really serious you will take the next step and find compelling reasons to keep going until you achieve the goal. These reasons will empower you and keep you focused when distractions come into play. Maybe your reason to become wealthy is to be able to buy your parents a home, or give your children a better life than you had, or maybe it is because someone was kind to you when you were down and out and you want to repay that kindness by helping others.

I don't know what your reasons may be, but I do know that people who have compelling reasons to reach their goals tend to achieve those goals more quickly and more fully than other people. It is good to want to create wealth, but if you can identify a compelling reason for doing so, it will have a powerful impact on your success!

Do you have goals? Are they written? What are your reasons? What are your whys? I recommend you answer these questions right now, and then take the necessary steps to start making these dreams and goals into realities. German philosopher Nietzsche said, "If you know the *why* of living, you can endure any *how!*" Make a decision to find your why!

I also want to share a technique I have used with some of my coaching clients when they have struggled to find their reason and have struggled to get compelling whys. I know that people enjoy receiving unexpected presents, but I also have found that people love to see the expression on the faces of their loved ones when they give them presents. Even the coldest, coolest people get some satisfaction from the impact of their giving. So I started working with my clients on four categories to help them structure their goals.

First I ask them to write their "Giving Goals." What would they like to give? What legacy would they like to leave? What impact would they like to have on the lives of others?

Next I help them understand that in order to "give," they must first "get," because you cannot give what you do not have! So I ask them to write their "Getting Goals." What do you need to get—what do you need to generate in order to give the things you would like to give? It is amazing that when we tie the getting to giving, it takes on more intensity than when we just want to get for ourselves.

I have found that most parents will do more for their children than they will do for themselves. They have things that they personally want, but they tend to do for their children first, then do for themselves. That is why it is good to know what our giving goals are before we work on our getting goals. What must you "get" so you can "give?"

The next category is the "Doing Goals." What must you "do" so you can "get" so you can "give"? This is when you start to map out your daily activities for generating more income. What steps must you take and what plans must you make? What must you do, and what things must you stop doing to achieve your goals? We all do things in our lives that are counterproductive to reaching our goals. (An example is when I said I wanted to lose some weight, yet I was eating ice cream at night...it was counterproductive to my goal, so I had to stop!)

Three major questions you must ask yourself: *What am I doing? What more could I do? What things must I stop doing to achieve my goals?* Once you know what you must do and what you must stop doing, you are on your way to greater success, and you will be clear about what you must do in order for you to get, so you can give!

Finally, what are your "Be Goals?" What must you be, so you can do, so you can get, so you can give? To do something you have never done, you must become someone you have never been!

- What must you become to be the person who can navigate the challenging economic seas and create greater wealth?

- What do you need to learn in regard to financial literacy?

- What books on business do you need to read?

- What new skill sets must you develop?

- What new habits must you cultivate?

- Who must you become in order to be the person who can achieve incredible results?

I believe we all have potential that is not yet tapped, and if we start to tap into that potential we will amaze ourselves. Ralph Waldo Emerson said, "What lies behind us and what lies before us are tiny matters compared to what lies within us." In the movie *The Lion King,* Mufasa says to his son, Simba, "My son, you are more than what you have become!"

I believe that there is more in us than we even know, yet we must be willing to constantly grow ourselves and develop ourselves. If we want greater results, we must be better; therefore, I am now learning Spanish and French so I can communicate with more people. I am exploring ways that I can continue to grow, and I implore you to continue to grow yourself and continue to develop yourself! What must you "be" so you can "do," so you can "get, so you can "give"? I truly believe that if you answer these questions you will see that your future will become clearer and much brighter!

BE PROACTIVE

*"Your future depends on many
things, but mostly on you!"*
—FRANK TYGER

To turn your finances around, it is critical that you become proactive. The word *proactive* was popularized by Dr. Stephen Covey in his landmark book, *The 7 Habits of Highly Effective People*. I first read his book years ago, but one year I had the opportunity to speak at the same conference with him in Australia, and we developed a friendship. I was able to learn in greater depth what he meant by *proactive*. To be proactive is to take anticipatory actions. Dr. Covey felt that all of his seven habits were important, but that being proactive was the bedrock habit—the foundation on which the other habits spring forth.

To be proactive is to recognize that your personal actions can have an impact on your present situation and change it for the better. Being proactive means you take action, not sit and wait. Being proactive means you are "up and doing" (as my mother used to say about people who were ambitious). Being proactive means taking responsibility for your future and being willing to move on your thoughts and dreams rather than waiting for them to manifest. You take the necessary actions to make those thoughts and dreams into realities, and think through the necessary steps required.

Being proactive is the opposite of being *reactive*, which means to wait for some outside stimulus to appear in order for things to change. Reactive people have a mindset that "this is just the way things are, and we cannot do anything to change them." Proactive people do not wait for things to happen, they make things happen! To turn your economic setbacks into greenbacks, it is necessary that you be proactive.

WINNERS MAKE THINGS HAPPEN, LOSERS LET THINGS HAPPEN

On my desk is a sign that states: "Winners make things happen, losers let things happen!" Some people state it a little differently; they say, "Some people make things happen, other people watch what happened, and then the rest stand around and ask, 'What happened?'" Whatever way you want to say it, the truth remains that those who are winners are those who make a determined decision to make things happen!

When asked what keeps them from being successful, most people will blame the government or the economy or their families or the "isms" of life (you know...sexism, racism, ageism, etc.). But the one thing that most people avoid in their list is that which is most important. It is the person they see every day in the mirror—it is us! We are the main obstacles to our success in life!

It has been stated, and I believe it is true, that success follows the 80/20 rule: 80 percent of the work usually comes from 20 percent of the people. In personal achievement, this means we are responsible for 80 percent of our failure to hit our goals, and outside obstacles are only 20 percent of the problem. An old African proverb states, "If you can overcome the enemy on the inside, the enemy on the outside can do you no harm!" We must be brutally honest with ourselves and come to the realization that we are the biggest challenge to our own success!

If you want to win, you must stop *letting* things happen and start *making* things happen. Remember, when all is said and done, much more is said than done...so let's go get it done! Today, make a commitment to overcome yourself, so you can reach your goals.

During tough economic times, some people sit and wait for the economy to change. They talk about how bad things are, and they just want to survive the storms. Yet there are others who do not wait for things to happen, they make things happen. Michael V. Roberts is one of those people. In fact, he has made things happen so successfully that he and his brother, Steven, now run a number of companies under the Roberts & Roberts banner that have a combined worth of almost $2 billion. He is a man who realizes that tough economic situations present big challenges, but also offer big opportunities.

I met Mike Roberts when I spoke at the A. G. Gaston Economic Conference in Birmingham, Alabama. He was the opening speaker and I was the luncheon speaker, so I arrived early to listen to his message. As I sat and listened to his story I was totally blown away.

Mike shared how he had grown up in the inner city of St. Louis, Missouri, with working-class parents "who were not poor, but just never had any money." He went to college and law school, and when he finished law school, he saw that St. Louis was in the midst of economic calamity. Many of the big industrial companies had shut down, and many of the houses were abandoned and boarded up. He started a small development company with his brother and also started working on changing the mental attitude of the citizens of the city. He was so successful that he was elected to a seat on the city council. Soon thereafter, his brother was elected to the city council as well. They kept working on projects to improve the city, and eventually their company grew so large that they had to commit all of their time to the company. They left the city council and started working on building more and more housing for the citizens of St. Louis.

The Roberts brothers expanded their business to include a construction company and then a media company when they were able to buy a small television station. They continued to grow both businesses and became one of the biggest developers and media companies in the country. They now own hotels across the United States, telecom companies, and airplane leasing services—all because they used a down and depressed economic situation to build a tremendous business.

Michael V. Roberts has written a book, *Action Has No Season,* which focuses on the fact that those who are proactive do not care about the time but know that there are always opportunities for those committed and determined to be successful. In the book he invented a new word, *actionaire,* which refers to people who do not wait for things to happen, but rather take action and make things happen!

Mike says that if you want to create wealth you must be willing to learn as much as you can about your particular business and then learn as much as you can about running a business and managing people and performance. He encourages people in his book to pursue wealth and not simply try to become "rich." He says that rich people tend to think in terms of one generation, while wealthy people think in terms of legacy, meaning that their wealth can be maintained and sustained over many generations.

Mike says that "rich people scream, while wealthy people whisper." He says that rich people tend to look and act like they are rich and stand out as being rich, while wealthy people tend to be understated in their wealth. And I think Mike is on to something because in the Bible, God tends to frown on being rich (consider the story of the rich young ruler and the parable about it being harder for a rich man to get into heaven than it is for a camel to go through the eye of a needle (see Luke 18:22-25). Yet God tends to smile on being wealthy! (Deuteronomy 8:18 states that it is God who gives you the power to get wealth and Proverbs 13:22 states that a good man leaves an inheritance for his children's children, but the wealth of the sinner is stored up for the righteous.)

Mike Roberts also says that when he and his brother started, they didn't have two dimes to rub together. They did not come from a wealthy family, but although they did not have much money, they had a dream and a willingness to work hard and invest the time and energy to get up and going. The Roberts brothers both agree that there will be challenges and setbacks, but you must keep a positive outlook and make up your mind that you are in it to win it! Start with a dream, work hard on your plan, and then take massive action! Be an actionaire and play to win!

TO BE PROACTIVE MEANS TO GET UP AND TAKE ACTION!

If you are going to turn your setback into greenbacks, then it is absolutely necessary that you take action. Jack Canfield, co-author of the best-selling Chicken Soup for the Soul series, shared with me that he and his co-author, Mark Victor Hanson, were turned down by more than 30 publishers, but they kept believing in their book and, therefore, they kept trying. Finally a small publisher, Health Communications, Inc. (HCI), took a chance on them and signed them to a publishing deal. HCI could not give them a big advance and could not promise massive distribution. The authors told HCI if it would just get the books *into* stores, then they would do the work to get the books *out* of the stores. They would hustle and work 24/7 to promote the books.

They went to work and made a commitment to do two radio or television interviews each and every day. They did this for over a year, and slowly but surely the books started to sell. Within a few years, they had a national best seller, then an international best seller, and then a second portion of Chicken Soup came out and it too became a best seller. And from there a multimillion dollar success story unfolded for Mark and Jack. You have to be proactive and take action.

Jack shared an example of how he shares the importance of being proactive with his audience. After talking about his challenges with creating his own success story and how he had to get up and take action, he pulls out a $100 bill and asks, "Who wants this one hundred dollar bill?" People wave their

hands and holler and scream at him, but he just holds the bill...
until someone gets up and comes up to the front of the room
and takes it out of his hand! That is the person who wins!

Author and success coach John Di Lemme says:

The winner—is always part of the answer.

The loser—is always part of the problem.

The winner—sees an answer for every problem.

The loser—sees a problem for every answer.

The winner—sees a green near every sand trap.

The loser—sees two or three sand traps near every
green.

The winner—says, "It may be difficult, but it's
possible!"

The loser—says, "It may be possible, but it's too
difficult!"

The winner—says, "I must do something!"

The loser—says, "Something must be done!"

Choose to be a winner!

GET UP AND GET GOING—FIND YOUR GOOD FOOT AND GET ON IT!

James Brown, the "King of Soul," had a popular song when
I was young that said, "Get up on the good foot...everybody
get up!" As we look at the process of creating wealth, I think

it is a good idiom from which to draw a conclusion about your success and wealth building. First, if you are serious about your success, you must make a commitment to *get up and get going.* Very little success comes to you unless you are involved in the process.

Author Bo Bennett said in his collection of quotes (*Year to Success,* Archieboy Holdings, LLC, 2004), "Confusing the words hope, wish, faith, and pray with each other usually just results in a minor grammatical faux pas, but when any of these words, especially hope, are confused with action, the results can be devastating!" Scripture says in James 2:26 that faith without works is dead. You must get up and take action on your goals and dreams!

Next, you should get on your good foot. Everybody has a good foot, the skill or gift with which they have been blessed. You must find your gift and be willing to use it. One of the keys to success and wealth building is to find your competitive advantage and exploit it. He said, imagine a 7-foot, 300-pound guy who decides to become a jockey because someone told him that was an option. It sounds silly, but every day we find people who listen to others about their future and never find or recognize their own natural gifts. Some people are good with art, others might be good with writing, others might be good with organization or analysis, and others might be good with cooking. I don't know what your "good foot" is, but I do know that everyone has something that comes easily to them. I recommend you find your good foot, get up on it, and get busy!

Let me say that occasionally life will throw you a curveball and take away that "good foot" option. For instance, maybe your company downsized or eliminated your position, and you are unable to find work. If for some reason you cannot get up on your good foot, I say get up on whatever foot you can until you can do better. As my friend Walter Bond, the former professional basketball player who was named Speaker of the Year by the Minnesota Tourism Association, says, "I got fired from basketball and realized I had to find a new love. So I went to work on me and found that I had other gifts and skills that I simply needed to work on and develop." I say, if you cannot get up on your good foot, get up on whatever foot you can get up on and get busy!

Dr. Stephen Covey popularized the word *proactive*, but it is not a new concept. People throughout the annals of time have found that taking action can have tremendous benefits on success and achievement. They just called it by different names. As I said earlier, my mother called it "being up and doing." Another phrase I have heard since childhood is "go-getter" or a "make-it-happen person." All these terms end up at the same place; that is, to change your present circumstances you must take action and work hard. I like to say that you've got to hustle!

UNDERSTANDING THE POWER OF HUSTLE

In terms of turning your setbacks into greenbacks, you must be willing to hustle. You decide to consistently work on your hustle muscle and develop it and make it stronger. As with any other muscle, the way to grow your hustle muscle is to exercise it, because the more you work the muscle, the stronger it gets. Just as if you wanted to grow your biceps you would exercise those muscles, so too must you exercise your hustle muscle. Develop it, strengthen it, and make it a muscle that works for you because you have made the decision to work on it.

I made a commitment to hustle when I started my speaking business, and have continued to hustle since day one. My friend James Carter, the Unstoppable Visionary, was a guest on my radio show and said, "Some people have a sales plan and a marketing plan, but very few have a hustle plan! Willie Jolley taught me the power of having a hustle plan!"

You might ask, what is a hustle plan? It is simply a determination that you will work harder than others think is necessary. You will do what is necessary to reach your goals, as long as it is moral and legal. You will not give up or give in until you achieve your goal. You will fight and keep fighting for your dreams!

I love what Bishop T. D. Jakes said about the power of hustle. He said that many people wonder where he came from and how he seemed to pop onto the scene. People do not realize that he struggled and scraped for 25 years in the back hills of West Virginia in order to become an "overnight" success. He said that he dug ditches to support his family while he was working on his craft, and preached to conferences where there were 25 people in the audience. He traveled around in an old, beat-up car, yet he refused to give up and continued to hustle. He said that when he dies, he recommends that you look under his fingernails, because you will find dirt there. Why? Because he never stopped scraping and clawing, even when he became famous.

I say that you must get a hustle plan, and it will take you places you never imagined you would go. Never forget the bridge that brings you across; it usually is the bridge that takes you to the next level.

Once I went to the National Association of College Activities Convention. They were choosing the speakers for the year. I could not afford the registration fee for the convention, so I called a friend who was starting to get some speeches at colleges, and I asked him to let me stay in his room.

Since I couldn't afford the registration, I went to the convention hall, stood outside, and gave out my little flyers about my speaking business. When my friend saw me, he told me, "Stop, man. That's not cool or sophisticated; it's embarrassing!" As soon as he left, I started giving out the flyers again. When he saw me again, he was angry. He said, "Man, this isn't how we do it. You're embarrassing yourself!" Yet again, as soon as he left I started back up, and continued until I had given out all of my flyers.

Later that day, I was walking near the convention center, and a man started hollering out to me. I thought he was a security officer and might have been upset because I had broken the rules by handing out my flyers outside the convention hall; but I decided to just deal with whatever he had to say. The man caught up with me and said, "Are you the guy who was giving out those flyers this morning?" I said, "Yes, I confess...it was me!" He said, "Good! I have been looking for you all day! I am the owner of the biggest college booking agency, and I think that if you have enough guts to hustle and work like you did today, then I think you will be a help to our agency." He went on to become my biggest booking agent for colleges! This happened because I was willing to hustle.

Abraham Lincoln said, "Good things come to those who wait, but only things left behind by those who hustle." I say, "Good things come to those who wait, but you have to hustle if you want to be *great!*" To create a growing business, you have to hustle! So go get busy...and hustle!

Be Aggressive!

When I was in high school, there was a cheer that we would all shout when our team was down and we wanted to fire them up. The cheerleaders would lead the cheer and then we would all join and shout it at the top of our lungs: "Be aggressive! Be aggressive! B-E A-G-G-R-E-S-S-I-V-E! Be aggressive! Be aggressive!" The chant would continue until our team responded, played harder, and turned the game around. In basketball, there is a defense that is often utilized when a team is down and trying to turn the game around. It is called a "full court press." It is a tactic used when the defense is super aggressive and has made the decision that they will no longer let things happen, but will instead make things happen. Similarly, if you are going to turn your setbacks into greenbacks, you will have to be aggressive!

Learn to Love Sales and Marketing

The next point of interest to turn your setbacks into greenbacks is to be more active in getting more people to know about you. It is critical for you to market, market, market, and sell, sell, sell. The old adage states that "Nothing happens until a sale is made!" You must be willing to sell your thoughts and ideas. Sell your products and services, and convince the marketplace that you have something of interest that can benefit them. I tell my staff that it is important to realize that people have pain and difficulty all around them, and our job is to sell them a solution to ease that pain. As noted speaker Jim Feldman said on my SiriusXM Radio show, "You must find someone's pain and then sell them an aspirin. You must first see the need, then fill the need with a solution. Once you have a solution to that need, then you can charge them a fee to apply the solution to their need!" In order to have serious success, you need to learn to love to find solutions and sell those solutions to those who need them. Selling is critical and is a major part of the process of turning setbacks into greenbacks!

A speaker friend called one day, and during the conversation he said, "You know, I love speaking, but right now we are having difficulty with our sales. I hate selling!" As soon as he said it, I knew why his sales were suffering. I told him, "If you ever want to have success in your life, you must sell. Therefore, you can never let those words come out of your mouth again. In fact, you can never let those words enter your thoughts! To have success, you must learn to sell your thoughts, your ideas, your products, or your services. And to sell them effectively, you have to learn to love selling!"

I told my speaker friend that I had learned a valuable lesson years ago, when I had just started traveling and speaking around the country. I was getting some name recognition and I was receiving invitations to speak all across the United States, so I was getting on and off planes every day. The travel was fun at first, but after about a year the traveling lost its glamour and I started to dread it.

About that time, I had a conversation with another speaker friend, Keith Harrell, the author of *Attitude Is Everything*, who was also traveling a lot. I said, "Man, I hate this travel!" He said, "Willie, you can never let those words come out of your mouth again, because whatever you speak eventually becomes your reality."

Keith then asked me a very poignant question, "Willie, what do you love to do?"

I replied, "I love to speak and inspire people."

He then said, "Do you agree that in order to do what you love you might have to travel occasionally, and that perhaps that really is the price you have to pay in order to do what you love?"

"Well...yes, I suppose that is true," I admitted.

Keith said, "Then you can never ever say again that you hate to travel, because travel is really just a price you pay to get to do what you love to do!"

I shared that story with my friend who had said, "I hate selling," and told him that he had to think differently. I told him that when I was in college, I took a logic class and I learned about deductive logic, which states that if Socrates is a man, and all men are mortal, then Socrates must be mortal. Going along the same line of thinking, if he loved to speak (which he told me he loved to do), and if selling was what he must do in order to speak more, then logic would say that therefore he loved selling!

He was quiet for a few seconds and said, "You know what, Willie...you are right!" He then proclaimed, "I love selling! I love selling! I love selling!" His sales started to improve, because his thinking improved and his attitude improved. He has gone on to build a very successful business and sell millions of dollars of products and services.

One of the points I share with audiences is that they must TTP, which means "Talk To People!" When I got started speaking, I had a 5-foot rule: If someone was within 5 feet of me, I was going to talk to the person. I remember a time when I stood at the subway in Washington, DC, and gave out my little "ugly" flyers. I call the flyers "ugly" because they were not fancy or professionally reproduced, but they were the best I could do at the moment. So I went with what I had to work with, because it was critical that I get my business going, and I needed to get it going quickly.

I stood at the subway and handed out those ugly little flyers. Some people looked at the flyers and then ditched them in the trash, but some took them and read them. A few weeks later, I got a call from a government agency and the woman on the phone booked me to speak for her organization. I asked her how she had heard about me, and she said that someone on her team had taken a flyer at the subway, and when they were looking for a speaker, they decided to use me. I believe that you must make a commitment to TTP. Let people know who you are and what you can do to bring value to the marketplace. Once you TTP, I recommend you TTMP—Talk To More People!

One of the marketing techniques I have used over the years is a technique I learned from one of my mentors, Joe Charbonneau. Joe was one of the early sales coaches in the speaking business, and he taught a sales technique called 13, 13, 12, & 12. He said that if I made 13 sales calls on Monday and 13 on Tuesday, then followed that up with 12 sales calls on Wednesday and another 12 on Thursday, and then sent out correspondence to all of those people on Friday—I would have made 50 new sales contacts that week.

It sounded so elementary that I wondered if it was enough; but when I actually got 13 conversations in a day, followed by 13 conversations on the second day, and then 12 conversations followed by 12 more conversations, it was amazing how my business started to grow.

I realized it was not just the fact that I was making the calls, but also that I was using a system. And many people have become millionaires because they followed a prescribed system for success—just as many people are able to lose weight on specific diet systems when they couldn't do it on their own. And the same is true for creating wealth—find a sales system that works, and follow it!

Another one of my buddies and frequent guests on my SiriusXM Radio show is Larry Winget. Larry Winget is a television personality who has been featured on TV in commercials for Hyundai and was also the star of the hit show *Big Spender* on the A&E network. He is also a *New York Times* best-selling author and Hall of Fame speaker. Larry Winget, was one of the first people I met when I started my speaking career, and we immediately connected because we were so similarly focused on marketing as a main way to build our brands and our incomes. Larry says that there are two, and only two, reasons why your business is not prospering. First, your product or service is not good enough, so you should continue to improve your product or service. Two, you are not talking to enough people who can purchase your product or service.

I agree with Larry that you need a good product and then you have to make a commitment to get the word out. You must talk to a lot of people or use technology to help you get your business's message to a lot of people. One thing for sure is that people cannot buy from you if they do not know you exist! So get busy and get the word out about your business, and you will be on the way to turning your setbacks into greenbacks.

To Be Outstanding You Must Stand Out!

If you are serious about becoming wealthy, you must stand out from the crowd and out-work and out-think your competition. Make a commitment to be distinct and build your brand. Best-selling author and speaker Scott McKain was a guest on my show and said that you just need to be 1 percent better than your competitor. Just commit to do a little more than your competition. Give a little more, go a little further, and try a little harder. Remember, the horse that wins the Kentucky Derby by a nose makes ten times as much as the horse that takes second place. Set yourself apart—get up, get busy, and hustle.

While I was speaking in Okinawa, Japan, for the U.S. Marines, a group of Marines took me out to dinner one evening, and I noticed a lot of bright neon signs. I asked about the places that had the bright signs and was told that those businesses were the casinos, and the bright lights were there to attract customers. My host said, "The bright neon lights attract customers just like lanterns attract bugs!"

Over the next few days, I noticed that the casinos did not only have bright lights, but they also had lots of signs and advertisements all around the island. And from what I was told, these businesses saw rapid growth once they started advertising. I realized there was a lesson in this action—businesses that grow most rapidly are those that understand the power of standing out!

In order to have an "outstanding business," you need to "stand out" from the crowd. Whether it's a casino with bright lights or a small business with a big ad in the newspaper, those businesses that grow most rapidly are those that understand the power of getting the word out about their organization! I have found a truism that applies here: it is hard to grow your business if no one knows you are in business.

If people don't know you are in business, they cannot call and therefore they cannot do business with you. Many people are working hard to grow their businesses but are missing a valuable tool for that job—advertising. I like what Ted Turner said about the secret to his business success: "Early to bed and early to rise...work like crazy and advertise!" Reader, I recommend you make a commitment to take advantage of the powerful business growth tool called advertising! The old adage is true: A business with no sign usually is a sign of no business! Do not be ashamed to let people know you are in business.

The Paradox of Risks and Rewards

Why is it that most people do not maximize their potential? The answer is fear! Fear is the number one reason people do not act on their thoughts and dreams. Fear will stop people in their tracks and make them stop trying. We must overcome our fears, or our fears will definitely overcome us.

You must take risks if you are going to turn your setbacks into greenbacks. The challenge is, what risk are you going to take? If you want to turn your setbacks into greenbacks, then you must get your economic engines going.

I have a few ideas that can help you manage risk. A few years ago I was invited to speak at High Point University in High Point, North Carolina, where my friend Nido Qubein is the president. Nido is not only the president of High Point University but also one of America's foremost business development experts. He is an award-winning speaker, a best-selling author, and a master businessman. If you are not familiar with Nido, I recommend you visit his Website: www. nidoqubein.com.

While visiting with Nido, I asked him about the secret to his amazing success. He said, "Brother Willie, the key is to understand that success is a result of making good decisions, and decisions always involve risk. Therefore, you must learn to take good calculated risks." Then he shared his risk management formula, which I want to share with you, because it is priceless.

Nido said that before you make an important decision, you need to ask yourself four questions:

1. What is the best that can happen if I make this decision?

2. What is the worst that can happen if I make this decision?

3. What is the most likely to happen if I make this decision?

4. Am I willing to live with the worst to get to the best?

When you answer these four questions, then you will get a very clear answer as to how you should proceed. When you get confirmation to the questions, then that is a good calculated risk, and you should move on it. If the answers are negative, then you should walk away without regret.

I realized as I read through the questions that they really are the definitive questions when you are faced with difficult choices. Thinking back to my decision to leave my job and start my speaking business 15 years ago, though I didn't know these four specific questions, I intrinsically went through the same process.

I was working in a job that I could not stand (and to show that I was part of the majority, some studies show as high as 87 percent of people get up and go to jobs that they really do not like). I was faced with the decision to stay in that job and have security, or leave the job and live my dreams. I thought about what was the best that could happen if I left my job. I realized that my dream was to make a difference in people's lives and in the process have some financial success and get to travel around the world. I then thought about the consequences and realized that the worst that could happen was to fail and possibly lose my house. Let it be noted that I realize losing my house is a pretty bad consequence, but I wouldn't die. And if I didn't die, I believed I could make a comeback! I realized that I would have to struggle, and that this quest would not be easy. I would probably have to work harder than I ever worked before. But as I looked at the scenario, it came down to a simple mindset: I was willing to fail at something that I loved rather than succeed at something that I hated.

Since I made that decision, more than 20 years have come and gone, and I am so happy I made those tough choices. I encourage you to use this formula so you can live your dreams and have greater personal and professional success. Just try it... it could change your life!

SPEAK POSITIVITY INTO YOUR FINANCES

I believe you must speak positivity into your life and your situation, even when things are not going well. I make a point to tell people to watch their language, because your language has an impact on your mindset and on the way life will respond to your situation. For instance, never say, "I am poor." Instead, say, "I am wealthy; I do occasionally have some cash flow challenges, but they are always temporary!" Remember that whatever you speak is what you attract, so speak in a positive manner and goodness will flow into your life!

I love visiting Australia, and one of the things I love most is when my Aussie friends say, "Good on you, mate!" What a great greeting. I have learned to say, "Good on you" to my friends, as well as to myself and my finances. Speak goodness into your life and your finances.

Success results for those who are willing to shift their thinking and look at life in its totality and not in segments. To shift from looking at life from a negative perspective to looking at life from a positive perspective, you must act on the new way of thinking. It is not easy to make the shift, but if you are willing to grow your thinking, grow yourself, and take action, then you can start to live life at another level. You must make that choice. You cannot always choose what happens *to* you, but you can always choose what happens *in* you! You cannot change the circumstances that life throws at you, but you can choose how you respond to the circumstances. My friend Tim Storey, who is a powerful evangelist and motivational speaker, says, "Challenge is a part of life. Your choices do not usually create your challenges, but your choices can usually get you out of your challenges!"

Many people say that they took a specific action because they had "no choice." They might say, "I gave up on my dreams or my goals because I had no other choice." I agree that although they might not have had a *pleasant* choice, they always have a choice. Will be it be easy? *No!* But is it worth it? The answer is a resounding *yes!* Just keep moving and keep growing and keep believing, and you will find, as I have, that the best is yet to come! Even in the midst of tough times you can turn your setbacks into greenbacks.

WHY DON'T YOU SAY YES?

I say that we must overcome our fears and learn to say *yes* to life and to success! Say *yes* to our dreams and *yes* to the life we have always wanted to live. Say *yes* to the possibilities and *yes* to the opportunities that are all around us. You might ask, "What possibilities?" I say that there are possibilities all around you, and if you only stop saying *no,* you will start to see that they are everywhere, especially in the United States. This is the land of possibilities; even in the midst of a recession, there are opportunities.

Have you noticed that people are still trying to immigrate to the United States? Have you noticed that people who come to America from other countries seem to do well? In fact, studies show that people from other countries become millionaires in America five times faster than people who were born here. Why? Because they might have come from a country where the average wage was $10 a day, and in the United States they can make $10 an hour. They come with a different perspective and a different mindset, and they come to America and say *yes* to success. They see money in places that people who were born in America overlook.

I recently had a conversation with friend Peter Tabibian, the owner of a new hamburger chain called Z-Burger. I met Peter at a 7-Eleven store where I often stop for coffee. He had seen me on television, and we talked about his life and his business. He said he came to America as a young man and has always been amazed by this country. He feels that the United States is the greatest country in the world because of the opportunities it offers. I asked him what impact the economy was having on his business, and he said that business was booming. He did say that it was harder than before, but not even close to as hard as it had been when he was growing up in his native land. He said that even in hard times, this was a great time and great place to do business. In fact, I came home from a trip a few weeks ago and turned on the evening news, and there was Peter with former President Bill Clinton, who had visited his restaurant to get some hamburgers. I encourage you to get a *yes* attitude to life and to your dreams. The possibilities are all around for those who are willing to open their eyes and their minds.

It is like the biblical story about the prophet Elisha and his servant Gehazi. The prophet Elisha kept forecasting the moves of the enemy and sharing this information with the generals of the army of Israel, who were then able to escape the enemies' traps. The enemy generals got so upset that they asked who the traitor in their ranks was. They were told that there was not a traitor in the ranks, but rather that the prophet Elisha was telling the army of Israel what was happening. The generals sent troops to the place where Elisha was staying, and when his servant Gehazi awoke, he was stunned to find they had been surrounded by enemy soldiers. Gehazi ran to wake up Elisha and asked him, "My Master, what shall we do?"

Elisha told him, "Do not worry! For those who are with us are greater than those who are with them!" I can see Gehazi now, looking at all the great numbers of enemy soldiers and then counting on his fingers: one, two of them against the enemy. But Elisha prayed and asked God to open Gehazi's eyes. And when his eyes were opened, Gehazi was able to see that the mountains were filled with horses and chariots of fire sent from the Lord!

I pray that you will say *yes* to success and *yes* to the possibilities, and that your eyes will be opened to see all the incredible opportunities around you. Open your eyes and then move forward on those goals and dreams, and make them into realities.

ARE YOU STILL WAITING FOR YOUR SHIP TO COME IN?

Many people speak about how they are waiting for their ship to come in. They patiently sit and wait for their break. I remember my days as a nightclub performer (before the days of *American Idol*), when I was always waiting for my "big break," waiting to be discovered. (I didn't realize then that most of the people in the nightclub were too drunk to discover their way out the front door.) I had always heard people say, "Just keep singing, sing real hard, and one day somebody will give you a break!" I kept waiting for my break, but it never came. Then I learned to stop waiting for my break and start making my breaks. I learned that success is a choice that you must make happen, not a chance that you sit and wait for. I love the old Chinese proverb that states, "He who waits for roasted duck to fly into his mouth waits a long, long time!"

I learned that the best way to grow your future is to first grow yourself. I started a program of self-development, and I decided that I was no longer going to wait for my breaks. I was going to make my breaks. I had a choice: I could continue to wait for my ship to come in or I could swim out to it. I decided to swim, and I am so glad I did, because some of my friends are still standing at the pier, waiting. Success is not a thing to wait for; it is a thing to be achieved! Make a commitment to be proactive about your success. Make a commitment to take action *today* on your dreams and goals. Make a commitment to read and listen to something positive and uplifting each and every day. (If you don't have a copy of my new *Money Making Music and Minutes*, I highly recommend you get a copy, because it works!) Get started today!

One more secret that I want to share for growing wealth concerns the power of negotiating. When you become a better negotiator, you can improve your bottom line, because at the end of the day, it is not always how much you make but how much you keep. Michael Soon Lee, author of *Black Belt Negotiating*, was a guest on my radio show and shared a powerful strategy for improving your net worth: learn how to negotiate better, so you can keep more of what you make. Mr. Lee says that Americans do not negotiate anything but car prices and home prices, but people from many other countries negotiate everything. He says that almost everything is negotiable if the circumstances are right. Either you can get a better price, or you can get more for your money.

In his book, Mr. Lee shares some great tips on the power of negotiating to improve your bottom line. First, get over your fear and trepidation about asking for a better price. If you do not ask for the discount, the answer is always "No!" Second, look at the negotiation from the vantage point of the other person. If you can, help them see how making a deal with you can help them grow their business. Third, do your homework on the other person. Fourth, once you make up your mind to negotiate, do not look only at getting a lower price, but also at other options, such as getting something else thrown in, or getting better payment terms. Maybe you can pay over time and get it for low (or no) interest.

Every penny you can save adds to your bottom line. Some people will feel that asking for a better price is a hassle, but if you save a few dollars here and a few dollars there, after a year you can have a lot of dollars in your pocket!

Get started today!

BE CREATIVE

The next step to turn setbacks into greenbacks is to be creative! Think about ideas and then act on those new ideas—that's what it is all about. I want to make sure you don't miss the definitive words that I used in the preceding sentence: *think* and *act*. To turn your situation around you must *think* and then *act*. To be creative takes a commitment to thoughtful action. You need to think about new ideas and new perspectives and then develop a plan to make those thoughts into realities.

I have heard the saying for years that when you need more money, it is not really a money problem but rather an idea problem. You must work on being more creative to turn your setbacks into greenbacks.

THE CREATIVE SHOESHINE MAN

In my book *It Only Takes a Minute to Change Your Life!*, I share a story that shows the power of being creative. There was a shoeshine man in a small rural town who was very good at what he did. He wanted to expand and grow his business, so he decided to go to New York City and set up shop. The people in his small town told him that he would never make it in New York City, but he had faith and left to go build his business. When he got to New York, he realized that the competition was fierce; there were shoeshine stands on just about every corner, but he was not deterred. He set up his stand and started looking to grow his business, but it was slow going because of the tremendous amount of competition.

One day, a busy executive left his office a few blocks from the stand of this young shoeshine man. As the busy executive walked in the direction of the young shoeshine man, he was approached by another shoeshine man who said, "Hey let me shine your shoes; I need to pay my rent!" The business executive said, "No thanks!"

He went a little farther, and another shoeshine man said, "Hey why don't you stop here and let me shine your shoes—I need the work!" Again, the man said, "No thanks!" He went by a third shoeshine man, then a fourth, a fifth, and a sixth before he finally approached the stand of our young shoeshine man. As he approached, the young man was counting: "...97, 98, 99, 100." The young shoeshine man stopped the busy exec and said, "Excuse me, sir, you are the one hundredth person to pass my stand. Today is my birthday, and I am so thankful to have another day to celebrate that I planned to give the one hundredth person who passed my stand a free shoeshine. Please allow me the opportunity to shine your shoes and show my gratitude for having another birthday!"

The busy exec was taken aback and said, "Wow. That's great! I'll take you up on your offer!" He climbed up on the shoeshine stand, and the young man went to work on his shoes. When he finished, the busy exec looked at his shoes; they looked brand-new. He said, "This is the best shoeshine I have ever had! Give me a bunch of your business cards; I am going to tell all my friends to come get their shoes shined here!"

The young man gave him a bunch of cards and thanked him for letting him shine his shoes. As the busy exec started to leave for his meeting, he turned around and said, "Hey, it's your birthday. What do you usually charge?"

The young man replied, "Five dollars, sir!"

The busy exec reached into his pocket and pulled out a $50 bill and gave it to the young shoeshine man, saying, "Happy Birthday!" The young man was ecstatic! He then looked to the heavens, then looked at the $50 bill, then looked back to the heavens and said, "...97, 98, 99..."

The lesson here is that you must be creative!

To turn your setbacks into greenbacks, it is critical that you take time to think. You must make it a planned part of your daily routine to simply take time for creative thought. I recommend you take time every day with a pad and a pencil or with your computer and start the thinking session by asking this question, "How can I increase my income today?" I caution you to make sure to have the word *how* at the beginning of that question—don't simply ask, "Can I increase my income today?" If you ask the second question, you are already behind the eight ball. Don't be plagued by the gloom and doom of the media and the negative reports about how bad the economy is, how many businesses are failing, and how people are losing their jobs at record numbers. Do not ask nor entertain the second question; rather, keep your mind and focus on the first question: *"How* can I increase my income today?" If you focus on the *how* question, you will be amazed at the ideas that your mind will generate.

Earl Nightingale made a recording based on *Think and Grow Rich* called *The Strangest Secret,* which became one of the best-selling self-help recording of all times. It was recorded in the 1950s, but it continues to be a top seller in the self-help industry today. In this recording, Earl Nightingale stated that most people are not successful in life, due to the fact that they simply don't think. Those who are willing to think differently are those who have the greatest success.

The Importance of Imagination

The importance of imagination was impressed on me as a youth when I had the opportunity to meet Muhammad Ali. I was visiting my grandmother in Philadelphia, and my mother got tickets to see Muhammad Ali during the taping of a local television show. I was so excited I didn't know what to do. I couldn't wait until it was time to go to the television studio. We even got front-row seats! The champ arrived and shook every-body's hand in the front row, and I was so excited because I could now go home and tell all my friends that I actually shook hands with Muhammad Ali!

I look back now and realize that shaking his hand was fine, but that would wash off. However, during the interview, he said something that would not wash or wear off. He planted a seed that grew as I grew, and helped to shape my thinking. During the interview, he was asked how he had revolutionized the boxing industry so that people flocked to see his fights. His reply was that imagination was the key to his success. He said, "You see, I learned a long time ago that being good was simply not good enough; you've got to have imagination and you've got to dream." Muhammad Ali developed a personality that people either loved or they hated. Those who loved him came to see him win; those who hated him came to see him lose. Either way, every seat was taken!

I learned something that day that will help me for a lifetime. I learned about the power of dreams. I learned that you've got to have imagination, and that you've got to be creative!

Not long ago, I saw a powerful commercial. It was a commercial that featured a little boy watching an old clip of Muhammad Ali after he had defeated Sonny Liston for the World Championship. The young Ali was shouting, "I shook up the world! I shook up the world!" Then the scene shifted with the same little boy sitting with an elderly Muhammad Ali. He looked the little boy in the eye and said, "Shake up the world! Shake up the world!"

I believe we are living in a time when we can do some incredible things, if we are willing to have some imagination. Now is the time to change our thinking and change our finances and our futures. Now is the time to shake up the world! So go get busy! Shake up the world!

The Power of Your Network in Building Wealth

One of the secrets to success in building your wealth is being open to ideas from others and making a commitment to build your network with people who are big thinkers. It is essential to build your network and be able to listen and learn from others. Henry Ford said, "I don't have to know all the answers. I just need to make sure I am smart enough to surround myself with smart people, and I must make sure I am wise enough to listen and learn from them."

I have learned that it is your network that often determines your network! Who are you hanging out with? Who are you talking to and sharing ideas with? Are they the type of people who encourage you, inspire you, and pour positive energy into you? Or do they discourage you, depress you, and zap your energy and your creativity? Who you hang with will be who you will become...good or bad. So make a commitment to hang with people who will inspire ideas and encourage your entrepreneurial spirit, because those people will have a major impact on helping you turn your setbacks into greenbacks. Your network will definitely help you grow your network. Life is not just about what you know, but it is also about who you know, and who knows you! This is why it is important to develop a network of people you know and who know you— and know what you can do.

Studies show that in tough times, 90 percent of jobs are obtained as the result of personal relationships. People get jobs by way of who they know, either directly or as a result of connections with others in their network. I hired my marketing manager because one of my best friends got her resume from his sister-in-law, with a recommendation about her work. He knew I was interviewing people to fill a marketing position, and he sent me the woman's information and told me he had gotten a good recommendation from his sister-in-law. On his recommendation, I interviewed her, and after a terrific interview process, I hired her.

There is a theory that there are only six degrees of separation between any two people in the world, yet I believe in this time of social networking that the separation is even less. The key is that you must develop the relationships and work on the relationships. One of the points I think you should focus on during tough times is stepping up your networking. You must be willing to network and develop relationships with other people. Start working on the relationship before you need it. Additionally, I recommend that you make a point of making a deposit in the relationship before you try to make a withdrawal. See what you can do to help others before you go back and seek help.

To turn your setbacks into greenbacks, it is essential that you expand your network and work on creating strategic partners. I encourage you to make a commitment to contact people in your network and look for ways that you can be of help to them (and they can be of help to you). It needs to be a win/win opportunity, because the best strategic alliances benefit both parties.

Don't Just Look for a Job...Make One! (Become the CEO of YOU, Inc.)

I recommend that you stop thinking like an employee who is just looking for a job and start thinking like someone who is running the company. And that means that you must start thinking like the CEO of YOU, Inc. One of the ways you can do this is with network marketing. Network marketing is when a product is distributed via personal networks rather than in stores. The money and effort that would typically go toward advertising the product on television or radio are reinvested in incentives for the people who are actually doing the selling. And those people sell the product or service by offering the products to people in their networks and offering people in the networks the opportunity to get involved in the business and make additional income by selling to their personal networks.

Some people have a negative impression of network marketing, yet they do not realize that network marketing has helped lots of people become millionaires. When times are tough and when personal economies are stretched and people are looking for creative ways to make more money, then network marketing is a wonderful turnkey way to start a business. Plus network marketing is a low-cost way to start a business enterprise with others helping you to become successful, because the more successful you are, the more successful they will become.

Some people believe that network marketing is a pyramid scheme or a sophisticated Ponzi scheme. Well, there have been some bad network marketing companies, just like there have been some bad traditional companies. Yet, the majority of network marketing companies are legitimate and excellent vehicles for creating personal wealth. Donald Trump, Robert Kiyosaki, and many other success coaches recommend network marketing as an incredible way to create wealth, and I am adding my voice to theirs. Over the years, I have had the opportunity to speak for hundreds of network marketing events, and I stayed in touch with many of the people I met at those events—many have become millionaires and super success stories. I believe network marketing offers people a tremendous opportunity to become independent business owners and to become wealthy.

Volunteer and Make Your Place

Another way I recommend is to look at volunteering to grow your wealth. It sounds like an oxymoron, but it is not.

I was on a plane and met a young man who told me he was frustrated; he had been sending out resumes and had not had any bites. I told him he might have to try something different: volunteer, and be so excellent that he would create an opportunity. I asked him if he had ever heard of Michael Baisden, the syndicated radio show host. He told me he had. I told him that Michael Baisden once worked for the Chicago Transit Authority. He wanted to be a radio host, but no one would hire him, so he volunteered to work for free to show what he could do. He went on to create the top-rated show in the city. From that beginning, he was offered and accepted a big contract and a national syndication deal. I recommended to the young man that he volunteer and be so exceptional that he would create a spot for himself.

I even decided to give Baisden's example a try. I wanted to expand my national radio presence, and volunteered to do Monday morning interviews on radio stations for the Radio One Network. I called radio stations across America every Monday morning, and did it for free. After the first ratings period, we found that the program was getting high ratings, so they offered me a longer segment on their SiriusXM station—and they paid me! I have since gone on to create one of the top-rated self-help programs on SiriusXM Radio. And it started by being willing to volunteer.

Now let me tell you the rest of the story about the young man I met on the plane. I received a note from him stating that he had decided to volunteer, and the results were fantastic. Not only did he get a job, but it was a job that paid more than the job he previously had. If you cannot get people to pay you, but you believe in yourself and in your dreams, I recommend you volunteer and be excellent. In fact, be incredible!

Develop a reputation for excellence, and you most often will create a spot for yourself. You will determine your own destiny! In my program An Attitude of Excellence, I emphatically state that excellence is always your best job security!

Why? Because it is...excellence always pays the best dividends over time. Therefore, strive for excellence.

"I've Tried Everything!"

Often I talk to people who are going through challenging times, and they will say to me, "I've tried everything!" I will then ask them, "Have you tried this? Have you tried that?" Typically they will say, "Ah, no I didn't think of that!" I respond by saying, "Well maybe you haven't tried everything!" I recommend you sit down with a piece of paper and a pen and write at the top, "How can I achieve x" (whatever you are trying to accomplish), and then think of everything you can. After you have exhausted your own thinking, I want you to ask some of the people in your network about ideas they might have. (By the way, if they say, "It can't be done," then you need to make it a priority to stop listening to them and start growing your network.) In other words, you must recognize that you may have done all you could think of, but that might not be everything. Keep thinking and keep looking for answers!

THE BEST IS YET TO COME!

In my book *An Attitude of Excellence,* I share a story that literally changed my life and helped me get a new outlook on life and success. I was a new speaker and I was struggling with my business. I was struggling to keep the phone on and keep the electric company from turning the lights off. It was tough, and I was hoping that someone would call and book me to speak so I could pay my bills. Finally, I got a call from an organization in Orlando, Florida. They booked me to come and speak for their conference. I was so excited that I was going to make some money that I could hardly contain myself.

I went to Florida and gave the speech, and they gave me a standing ovation. I was on cloud nine! I got my check, and they even enclosed a small bonus for doing a good job. I got on the plane to go back home full of excitement because I had gotten paid. But then I started thinking about all my bills and expenses, and I realized that the money was already accounted for. It was allocated to everyone but me! All of a sudden I got depressed because the money was gone before I got a chance to even deposit it in my account.

As I sat there having a pity party with myself, I started talking to an older gentleman across the aisle. He must have sensed that I was struggling, and during the conversation he asked me a question that would have a profound impact on my life. He said, "Young man, how old do you think I am?"

I looked at him and I said, "Well, I would say you are about 60."

He smiled, took off his glasses, looked me right in the eyes, and said, "Young man, I travel around the country speaking to people about health and wealth, and I do it every day. And I want you to know that I am 88 years old, and my best is yet to come!"

In that moment, everything changed for me! If an 88-year-old man could see that his best days were in front of him and not behind him, what in the world did I have to whine and cry about? If an 88-year-old man could have that kind of optimism, what was keeping me from my success? The answer was that the problem was me. I was waiting for success to come to me rather than going out and creating success for myself. Rather than waiting for people to call me, I needed to call them. Rather than sitting in front of the fireplace shouting,

"Give me heat," I needed to put something in the fireplace to create some heat.

As I left the plane that day, I was a new person. I went home with a new attitude and new optimism. I got on the phone and started making sales calls and started to talk to more people about my business, and things started to change. That old gentleman was absolutely right—the best was yet to come!

Many years have gone by since that man spoke those words into my life and encouraged me, and a lot has happened. I have had success as a speaker, success as an author, and success with radio and television, yet I believe that this is just the tip of the iceberg of what is possible. I truly believe the best is yet to come!

And I believe that your best is yet to come! The question is, do you believe it?

Step 7

BE PRAYERFUL

The last step should be the first step, because it is actually the most important step, and that is to be prayerful. I have found that prayer changes things and gives you hope. A study from the American Psychological Association states that people with faith tend to live longer. I am amazed that when I interview people who are in their 90s and 100s and ask them their secret to long life, I always hear as one of the steps, "Have faith and trust God!" I learned years ago that if you want to know how something is done, go ask someone who has done it and learn from them.

Even though prayer is the most important step, I purposely put it last because far too often people misinterpret Scripture and think that if they pray, they don't have to do anything else. They have a theology that believes that they need not do anything but pray, and everything will be okay. Yet Scripture clearly states that if people do not work, they shall not eat! And it encourages people over and over again to pray and then to get up and go to work. Therefore, I purposely left this as the last step because I want to help people who are waiting for God to drop help in their lap, to get up and get going to help themselves.

My friend Wally "Famous" Amos, the famous cookie man, told my radio audience, "If you want God to drop something in your lap, it is best to put your lap where God is dropping stuff!" The great American statesman Benjamin Franklin wrote, "God helps those who help themselves." Even though many people think the quote is from Scripture, it not scriptural, but I certainly believe it has truth. I encourage you to pray and have faith, and to use your faith by acting on it! Scripture says, "Faith without works is dead." To turn setbacks into greenbacks, you must pray—then move your feet!

Over the years, I have encouraged my friends and clients to understand the three F's of Financial Success—*Faith, Focus, and Follow-through.* You must have *faith* that you are going to live your dreams and achieve big goals. Faith is the substance of things hoped for and the evidence of things not seen (Hebrews 11:1). In other words, faith involves the stuff that comes from having hope and believing that your thoughts and dreams can come true. It is walking and moving forward with the confidence of positive expectations—faith to expect good things to come from your actions and to see things in your mind that are not yet a reality as possible. My friend Dale Smith Thomas told my radio audience that F.A.I.T.H. is the opposite of F.E.A.R. Fear is False Evidence Appearing Real, while Faith is Finding Answers In The Heart! God asks us to have faith, and if we would just have the sincere faith of a mustard seed, we would be able to move mountains! If you are going to do incredible things with your life and have massive success, it is going to take faith!

Next you must have *focus.* Success is not about hocus pocus, but rather about focus! You must focus on your dreams and goals and not be distracted by all the noise and static that is constantly trying to take you off course and off target. That is why I have been shouting over and over again about the importance of goals and why you must take time to think about them, write them down, and then read them regularly! From the moment most people get up until the moment they go to sleep, they are being bombarded by a constant barrage of advertisements and messages from others that can take their focus away from their goals and dreams. It is like the siren song that will pull us off course. Sometimes you have to stop and turn off the world and focus for a moment on your dreams and goals and what it will take to achieve those goals.

Next is *follow-through,* which is the step that involves actively going through the business development process. I say that you must go through the process, because it is a part of the circle of life that you have a beginning, a middle, and an ending of all actions. I learned years ago when I started playing tennis that you must start with setting up for the swing, then you must swing and hit the ball, then you must follow through. If I didn't complete one of those first two steps, I would not get the shot across the net, and when I didn't finish the shot with a follow-through, the shot was weak and ineffective. Then, years later, I started playing golf and the instructor said the same thing: start by setting up, then swing the club and hit the ball, and then follow through. One day at a tournament, I forgot to follow through, and all of my shots were going all over the place. A friend stopped and looked at my swing and said, "Willie you are not completely following through on your shots!" I stopped and thought about it, and realized he was right. So

I tried again with a full follow-through, and the results were dramatically different. I was back in the game because I was willing to follow through on what I had started.

I have found the same thing to be true in the success process. You must set up and prepare for the necessary actions that will get you moving in the direction of your goal. Then you must take action—committed, consistent action. Then you must follow through and finish what you start. Follow through on the items you said you would follow through on, because your word must always be your bond, and if you say it, then you must do it! You must follow through on your calls and emails and business communications. The wealthiest people I know always find a way to follow through and communicate with people who want to do business with them. You must follow through on the items you have written down on your lists, and the steps to success you have developed.

After you do the three F's for Financial Success, I want you to add the three P's to Prosperity—*Pray, Plan, and Pursue!* First you should be humble enough to take time to *pray,* because prayer changes things. Prayer leads to hope, and you need hope to succeed, especially in challenging times. Scripture says, "We know that tribulation produces perseverance, and perseverance, character and character, hope" (Romans 5:3-4). You must have hope, and prayer will lead to hope! Don't be too proud to pray because prayer can empower and strengthen you for the journey.

Bruce Wilkinson wrote a book some years ago called *The Prayer of Jabez.* It shared the story of a man named Jabez who prayed that God would enlarge his territory, and God granted him what he requested! Why? Because Jabez was willing to trust God and pray for greater prosperity! Pray for what you want and be willing to ask God to bless you, and remember it is God who gives you the power to get wealth, yet it is up to us to be good stewards and to use our blessing to establish His covenant, and to help others. First pray! Remember, prayer gives you hope and the power to keep going, in spite of the challenges.

THE POWER OF HOPE AND PRAYER

It all comes back to prayer. Prayer is an important element in the comeback process, because prayer takes faith, faith creates hope, and hope creates optimism and a willingness to keep going, even in challenging times. Hope is the fuel for the journey, the element that will sustain you when everyone else gives up. You must have hope and high expectations to maximize your possibilities, because hope and expectation are powerful tools in surviving tough times.

The late, great speaker John Alston shared a story with me about the impact of hope. He said that a science club placed four frogs in a vat of water. They kept the frogs in that vat of water until they were almost out of air, and at the last moment they pulled the frogs out. The next day, they put those same four frogs in a vat of water, and they put four new frogs in a separate vat of water. They kept all the frogs under water until they were almost out of air, and then held them an additional 15 seconds. The new frogs, which had not been through the previous experience, gave up and died; but the four frogs from the day before held on and lived. The old frogs had hope and optimism and a belief that they would get through the challenge, because they had been through the earlier experience. Hope will have a high impact on your ultimate outcomes.

Next you must *plan!* Plan your work, and work your plan! If you want to create wealth, it is critical that you plan. Your plan can be fluid and flexible, but you need to have a business plan and an action plan. No great building was ever built without a blueprint, and no great army wins without a battle plan. You too should have a plan. You might have to make adjustments and changes as you go along, but at least you will know where you are going. Along with planning, you must position yourself so you are ready when the economy comes back. Wayne Gretsky said that the key to massive success was always positioning. He said, "A good hockey player plays where the puck is. A great hockey player plays where the puck is going to be!" Successful people position themselves where the money is going to be, not where it is now. Get in position now for the comeback!

Finally you must *pursue,* to go after it with all your might! Most people are waiting for their ships to come in, but the wise ones are swimming out to their ships. I will say this over and over and over again: First you must pray, and then you must get up and go to work. When you get red hot on your goal and pursue it, I believe you will find that things will start to happen that you could not imagine. If you want wealth in your life, you need to make the commitment to pursue. Pray, and then move your feet.

ARE YOU THE ONE TO OVERCOME THESE TOUGH TIMES?

In my twelfth-grade year, I had an experience that changed my life and gave me a new perspective. I had been messing around in school and just getting by. One day, while

I was in homeroom, there was an announcement on the public address system that said, "We have a motivational speaker who will be giving a presentation this morning, and everyone must attend!"

I told my teacher, "I don't need to hear a motivational speaker. I want to stay here in homeroom and do my homework—it's only two weeks late!"

She said, "Young man, you really need some motivation!"

I didn't want to go to the assembly that day, but I went because it was mandatory. I went to the auditorium and sat in the back row and threw my hood over my head and decided I was not going to listen. Yet, somewhere in his message the speaker got my attention. He said, "Someone in this room has something special inside. Someone in this room is going to do great things with his or her life. I don't know which one it is but I know for sure that it is one of you!"

In that moment something woke up inside me, and I heard a voice saying, "It's me! I'm the one!"

When the speaker finished, he walked off the stage and walked up the center aisle. He came right toward my row and I ran to the edge of the row and said, "Excuse me, sir!" He stopped and looked me in my eye and I wanted to tell him that I was the one he was talking about, but the words would not come out. I tried and I tried, but the words would not come out! Finally he nodded his head and told me to have a good day. As he walked away, I was so upset because I couldn't get the words out. At the same time, I was excited because something inside me had changed.

Years went by. While making a transfer in the Denver airport, I was walking from one gate to the other gate when, all of a sudden, I saw that man! I hadn't seen him since high school. I got weak in the knees, but I pulled myself together and walked over to him. I said, "Excuse me, sir. I am sorry to disturb you but my name is Willie Jolley and I need to ask you a question."

He said, "Are you Willie Jolley, the author and speaker? I have seen you on television, and I have read your books. I have enjoyed your work!"

I said, "Thank you, sir, but that is not why I stopped you. I need to ask you a question. Did you come to Roosevelt Senior High in Washington, DC, in the mid-1970s and speak to the students?"

He said, "Yes, I did."

I asked, "Do you remember telling the students that someone in the room had something special inside?"

Again he responded, "Yes, I do remember."

I then said, "Sir, I couldn't tell you then, but I can tell you now...it was me! I was the one you were talking about!"

I have found as I travel around the world that many times, when I am speaking to students, I get a sense that someone in that room has something special. Someone in that room has a reason for being there. They are supposed to do something great with their lives. I don't know who it is, but I do know it is someone in that room.

Today, I decided to write this piece because I have a sense that someone reading this book has something special inside of him or her. Someone has something awesome inside. This person came this way because he or she is supposed to do something incredible in his or her life. I don't know who it is, but I believe it can be you! Are you the one?

FAITH WITHOUT WORKS IS DEAD!

You must not only have faith but you must use your faith! You should not just think of your faith as a noun but also act as if it were a verb, something that you are acting on! When you act on your faith you are empowered to see that the words are real and the Scriptures can bring new energy and excitement to life! Faith is not something that we should read, but something we should live...on a daily basis. Today I want you to move on something you have been thinking about but have been afraid to try. Trust God and move now! Call out to those mountains in your life and tell them to get out of your way! Speak it with confidence and assurance and trust! It is truly by your faith! The measure you live and the measure you give is the measure you get! Move now!

It's by Your Faith
by Willie Jolley and Brian Taylor

Now as I read the Scriptures,
More and more I found this promise of power
That was given to us if we would just have faith.
The more I read, the more I found
That as you believe, so shall you receive.

Then I learned a little more
It says all things are possible
If you can just believe.
Then it said if a man believeth in the heart
So as he is. And I read a little more.

It said you achieve not, because of your unbelief.
Wow! And then we found we could have
Mountain moving faith, we could change our circumstances

Change our lives by the power of our faith.

It said for assuredly if you have the faith of a mustard seed
You will say to this mountain move from here to there
And it will move and nothing will be impossible to you.
I said Uh Oh I'm on to something here.

It said whosoever, (and I thought I was a who-so-ever)
It said whosoever says unto this mountain be removed
And be ye cast into the sea and does not doubt in his heart
But believes that those things he says will come to pass
He will have whatever he says.

Or if you have the faith of a mustard seed
You can say to the mulberry tree be pulled up by the roots
And it be planted in the sea, and it will obey you.

Oh I thought I was onto something then.
And I said okay what else can I learn
And it said ask and you shall receive
Seek and ye shall find.

Knock and the door will be opened unto you
For everyone who asks receives, and
everyone who seeks finds
And everyone who knocks the door
will be opened unto them.
Therefore most people receive not because
they either ask not, they seek not, or they knock not
And then they wonder why not!

You must have faith. It's as simple as that
Folks you got to have faith.
You got to walk by faith,
Talk by faith, live by faith, move by faith.

Oh, act on your faith.
You got to go out and understand that
you can move mountains.
You can achieve incredible things
If you're willing to step out on your faith.
Keep it! Keep the faith!

© 2004 B. Taylor Music Publishing (ASCAP)/Willie Jolley Music (BMI)

CONCLUSION

In life there will be setbacks, downturns, and challenges—not maybe, not might, but definite setbacks and problems. Yet it is important to remember that this is not personal, and it is not permanent. This too shall pass! Everyone feels the pinch of a recession or community economic downturn; it is an equal opportunity pain. Then everyone will at some point or other in their lives experience their personal economic situations, where they have their own recession or downturn. Yet in every burden there is a blessing, and if we are wise, it is out of these challenges that we can grow our wealth and success.

Recessions and depressions always lead to progressions. History has shown that out of each severe economic downturn, we became stronger as a country and our economy expands. After each economic downturn, we see greater increase in the general standard of living, and more people learn about wealth building and join the ranks of the millionaires. The key is that when you are at the bottom, it is critical that you do not give up hope but maintain a positive mindset. If you are willing to think about possibilities and if you stay positive, even in the midst of extreme challenges, you will realize that you can turn this around, and you can be the victor and need not be the victim! It is in these moments of challenge that we will either move forward toward our goals and dreams or we will fall back toward our fears. The choice is up to you!

So I close this book with these thoughts: Whatever you do, hold on to your dreams. This is not the time to give up and throw in the towel! This is not the time to quit! Tough times do not last, but tough people do! You must not just go through these tough times—you must grow through these tough times!

We stand at a time when it is up to us to make the most of this moment and to take advantage of the opportunities that are all around. Yet, wherever there are opportunities, there will also be challenges, and I pray that we will not only be fit and able to meet those challenges but to conquer those challenges and move to greater levels of success. I wish that you grow and stretch this year beyond what you thought you could do!

So I implore you to think big and make a commitment to focus on the positive and not all the negative gloom and doom. I believe that the best way to predict the future is to create the future, and so I believe this is going to be an incredible year! So get up, get dreaming, get going, get stretching, and get to really living life at another level! I pray that you work hard, work smart, and trust God! And finally, I pray that you prosper and be in good health, as your soul prospers!

Remember, you very well are *the one!* Live your dreams— and know that your best is yet to come.

God bless you!

BONUS MATERIAL

I am blessed to have some of the greatest people in the world as guests on my *Wealthy Ways* radio show. I am grateful for all the people around the world who have made my show part of their weekly routine and share the information with their friends and family.

I am constantly inspired and encouraged by the notes I get from listeners who share how the interviews have changed their lives. Some share how they have started businesses and grown their wealth, and others share how they have been encouraged through the interviews to not let life's setbacks stop them.

I decided to take a few of the top stories and comeback lessons that I have gathered over the years and create this special bonus material for you to enjoy. After compiling the information, I shared it with my editors and they felt it was the start of a new book series.

So get ready for a new book to come from the interviews that I have garnered over the years. This is the first edition, which will focus on people who had setbacks, turned them into amazing comebacks, and worked them into financial green-backs. These stories are real-life examples of how possible it is for everyday people like us to turn setbacks into comebacks, and eventually into massive amounts of greenbacks.

In addition, I have created a new program called *Walk with Wealth: The Interviews of the Willie Jolley Wealthy Ways Show.* I have found that you become who you hang out with, and if you want to be great and do great things, you need to hang out with great people so you can learn from them. Unfortunately, most people don't have access to great people in real life...but now you do through these interviews. You can actually walk with the wealthy via these interviews! The people I have interviewed have had a profound impact on me and positively changed my life. I believe these interviews will do the same for you!

In the material to follow, I have highlighted lessons of ten people who truly epitomize turning setbacks into amazing comebacks, and later into greenbacks. These are people who are no different from you or me—so please remember, "If they can do it, so can you!"

Please visit www.williejolleyradio.com to listen and access the actual interviews.

THE "FAMOUS"
WALLY AMOS

I first met Wally Amos in 1995 when we spoke on the same program, and I was excited to meet the famous cookie man. I had read Wally's books and seen him on television, but this was my first opportunity to hear him speak in person and witness his positive energy in real life. He did not disappoint! After that event, we sat and talked and shared ideas.

We immediately clicked, and over these many years we have remained friends. In fact, when he celebrated his 75th birthday, he decided to come to Washington, DC, to celebrate it with my wife and me, and we threw him a big birthday party!

Wally originally became famous by creating the delicious chocolate chip cookie brand "Famous Amos' Cookies." Unfortunately, through bad business decisions, he lost his company *and* lost the use of his "Famous Amos" name. He could go on using Wally Amos but due to some papers he signed, he could not use "Wally Famous Amos" in his branding, because the new company owned the recipe, the labeling, and the name! Yet, he refused to give up!

He continued to work on new projects and ideas. He moved to Hawaii and started working on his next big business venture. He started speaking more and telling people his story, and he never let his setback make him negative or bitter. He continued to share his positive energy and greet everyone he met with his big smile and "Aloha" greeting. He said that God gave him Famous Amos and God would give him another big idea.

He has since started a new cookie company that is taking off across the country. It is called The Cookie Kahuna cookie company and he is continuing to make cookies that are full of love and flavor, as he did with his original chocolate chip cookie. In addition, today Wally is a successful TV personality, entrepreneur, and author who continues to amaze me with his unstoppable attitude and energy. I have written about him in all of my books because he truly is an inspiration to me and I know his message will be an inspiration to you!

Here are some lessons to learn from the famous Wally Amos:

1. Success in life is the result of a series of tests. You must first take a test; once you pass that test, you proceed to the next level. When you get to the next level, there will be new tests waiting for you. Remember, if you stay in faith you will be well ready to meet all of the tests that you encounter.

2. All great things start with an idea! Therefore, there is immense power in your ideas. Write them down. THEN bring them to life.

3. God is not a one-idea God. If your first idea does not succeed, do not give up. God has many more for you. Strong and enthusiastic faith truly can move mountains, so stick with your dreams and never give up.

4. If you succeed once, it should give you a mindset of hopefulness that you can do it again.

5. You are always surrounded by opportunities. Yet, you must wake up, see the opportunities, and act on them.

6. Fulfillment in life is about doing more, being more, and achieving more—no matter how old you are!

7. A positive, "Yes, I Can Attitude" is a critical part of the success equation.

8. "Yes, I can" leads to "Yes, I will," and then you are on your way to something big! Many people can, but very few people will. Be the one who dares to dream and dares to do!

9. Persistence and perseverance are keys to success. You will succeed if you do not quit...so whatever you do, do not quit!

10. Decide to be unstoppable! If you stop, it's over. But if you keep going, everything is possible!

11. Total success comes from service to others. You become better as a result of better service. An attitude of service creates miracles!

12. Become a quality person who always gives your best to every job you touch. The big secret is that there is really no secret to success. You must work hard, have faith, stay positive, and serve others!

LES BROWN, THE MOTIVATOR!

Leslie Calvin Brown was born in an abandoned building in the toughest area of Miami, Florida, with his twin brother, Wesley. As infants, a lovely woman named Mamie Brown adopted the twin boys. She didn't have much money but she had a lot of love. Les grew up in poverty and was a terrible student. He flunked two grades and was labeled Educationally Mentally Retarded (EMR). As Les went through school he was routinely teased and called the DT (Dumb Twin).

During this time Les had low self-esteem and started thinking that the only job he would be able to get after high school would be as a trash man for the sanitation department. Yet one day while visiting the class of one of his friends, the teacher asked him to answer a simple math equation. Les told the teacher that he could not answer because he was the DT. The teacher came from behind his desk and said, "Never say that again! Someone's opinion of you does not have to become your reality!" The teacher encouraged him and inspired him to ignore the negative naysayers and start to believe in himself.

Les continued to grow his self-esteem and possibility thinking. One of his dreams was to be a disc jockey on the radio, because he loved the way they could spin the music and also spin their words with such flair. After the positive words from the high school teacher, Les decided to pursue his dream. He went to the local radio station to try and get a job, but was soundly rejected because he had no experience. But he did not let that rejection stop him, he kept going back. Day after day he returned and kept getting rejected, but he refused to give up on his dreams. Les persisted and was eventually hired as a "boy Friday," running errands, sweeping floors, and doing other menial jobs, while always preparing his mind for an opportunity to get into the DJ seat and spin the music and spin his words to fire up the listening audience.

Late one evening, the late-night DJ showed up drunk. He was too inebriated to work. And Les was the only other person in the building. The station manager called and asked Les if he could spin the records and temporarily replace the drunken DJ.

Les moved the drunken DJ out the way, sat down in the chair, and went to work. His mental preparation allowed him to not just be good, but to be excellent! He went on the air that evening and a new radio star was born! He became one of the most popular DJs in Miami, and later in Columbus, Ohio. After many successful years on the air, Les won a seat as an Ohio state assemblyman. As a result of his political status, Les started giving speeches and eventually became the #1 motivational speaker in Ohio, and within a few years, the #1 motivational speaker in America! He is now considered one of the top motivational speakers in the world!

Toastmasters International has named Les Brown "Motivational Speaker of the Year" and "One of the Top Five Speakers in the World." He has been inducted into the National Speakers Association Hall of Fame and received its prestigious Golden Gavel Award.

Today Les is a best-selling author, radio personality, and television star. Even though he never went to college, he has been invited to lecture at Harvard, Oxford, and many of the other great universities around the world. He often says that he does not have a college degree, but he has an MBA...a Massive Bank Account! He is considered a genius in speaking; and as a result of his excellence in communication, he has become one of the most successful speakers of all times. He went from failing in school and thinking he could only become a trash man to becoming a global success coach and business icon!

Here are a few life lessons from "The Motivator," Les Brown:

1. 1. Someone's opinion of you does not have to become your reality. It is *your* choice, not theirs!

2. Develop your mind to attract the money. In other words, develop your mind and you will develop the mindset that will attract the money!

3. O.Q.P. — Hang out with Only Quality People! Who you hang out with is who you will become!

4. Develop your communication skills, for when you open your mouth you tell the world who you are!

5. Think big and bold. What you think about, you can bring about!

6. Invest in yourself. There is a direct correlation in the books and programs you read or listen to, and the amount of money you make!

7. Expand your skill set. You must expand or become expendable! You get paid for the present value you bring to the marketplace. Remember this: used-to bees do not make honey or money!

8. Speak life, not death; blessings not curses! Your words create your reality! Make your conversations positive, productive, purposeful, and profitable.

9. Develop collaborative relationships and strategic alliances to help you achieve your goals, while helping others achieve theirs.

10. Help someone else, and help yourself, because what you give is what you get.

11. Don't settle for average or even good performances. To truly succeed you must pursue excellence. Make the commitment to stand out from the crowd with greatness and you will be handsomely rewarded.

12. Make a point to discover your purpose; when you do, you will not only make a good living, but you will make a positive difference in this world and love every second you are doing it.

DAVE YOHO,
THE AGELESS WONDER

Dave Yoho was born during the great depression of the 1930s. He experienced extreme difficulty growing up during America's Great Depression. His parents struggled to put food on the table and never achieved the American Dream of home ownership. As a young man Dave resorted to prize fighting and physical labor to make ends meet. However, he never let his circumstances determine his future. Instead, Dave made a decision to develop his mind and work on his business skills.

Today, Dave Yoho is an icon in the motivation and consulting industries. He gave his first speech when he was 23 years of age, and over the past 63 years he has given over 5,000 paid speeches. He is now over 85 years young and is still working daily, with the vigor and vitality of someone half his age. Even now Dave is still in high demand as a speaker and consultant. And he has made millions of dollars doing what he loves!

The dynamic, ageless wonder Dave Yoho shares these tips:

1. Age is a number, and you can choose how you look at that number. You can act like most people your age traditionally act, or act like someone years younger—and neither way is wrong. It truly is your choice!

2. In the book *A Tale of Two Cities,* the first line states, "It was the best of times, it was the worst of times...." That is true. You decide whether it is the best or worst for yourself! Your thinking and your attitude make the difference!

3. We live in a world focused on bad news, yet the good news is that most of the bad news is about perspective rather than truth. If you think things are bad, they will be. Yet, if you think things are great, so too will they be! Life is about perspective and choice.

4. Those who win most are those who think in "alpha" stage, which is a mindset of "This is just the beginning." No matter how old you are.

5. Learning is fundamental to long-term success. In times of great change, those who are the learners are those who craft and control the future.

6. If you want to stay young, you must stay active! Your central nervous system is fired by activity. Keep working, keep active, and you will keep living!

7. If you know what to do to be a success and you do not do it, then it is like not knowing it at all. So, do the good you know!

8. The EPOD Formula for Success works! Energy — Persuasion — Optimism — Discipline. Of all of these, optimism and discipline are the most important.

9. Ask yourself daily, "What have I learned?" Then ask yourself, "What will I do with what I learned today?" This will help you optimize information and personalize its usage to your journey to success.

10. Make the decision to be grateful. It is a choice and brings longevity to your success.

DUKE GREENE, THE MONEY MAGNET

Duke Greene was born and reared in the rural American south and learned about making money from his father and grandparents, who were entrepreneurs. His grandparents told Duke that he should always be excited about making money and making the money grow and work for him.

Duke took their words to heart and went to work as a young boy to make money. He earned money cutting grass, helping his father clean up his store, and assisting his grandmother in making quilts that she sold for a profit. He would then loan money to his friends and get a little interest when they paid him back. Duke learned that a person could make money by being creative.

When Duke went to college, he continued to earn money by cutting guys' hair in his dorm room and driving a trash truck after school. After he made the money, he loaned some to friends and got interest on the returns. He also invested in small businesses on campus that would buy snacks for cheap and then sell them at a profit on campus. After graduation,

Duke started a number of companies. One of those companies became America's first large African American-owned IT company, International Business System (IBS). Duke started IBS with $500 and built it into a multimillion dollar enterprise with more than 600 employees. Later he expanded to other services and earned multimillion dollar contracts for training, travel, logistics, and gas/energy deployment.

In the 1970s, Duke had a beautiful office on the tenth floor of a prestigious Washington, DC, office building, which faced the White House. He was featured on the front pages of numerous business magazines as America's best new CEO. His company was making tens of millions of dollars and Duke was living the good life. Then the economy tanked during the recession of the 1970s. Gasoline was limited and people had to wait in line to fill their cars with gas. Plus, people were being laid off from their jobs in large numbers. It was a tough time for businesses in America.

Duke's business was especially impacted due to his work with gas and energy. On top of this, he had recently hired some of the best and brightest energy experts in the country. Duke did not want to lay them off and potentially lose them to his competition. So, he decided to take his personal salary as the CEO and put it all into the employee pool, making sure that his staff continued to get paid.

Duke continued this pattern for many months and paid his personal bills out of his savings. After some months his savings were completely depleted, so he had to do what was necessary to pay his personal bills. Every day Duke went to the office at 8 a.m. and worked as the CEO until 6 p.m. Then he grabbed something to eat, and from 8 p.m. until 3 a.m. he drove a trash truck to earn money to pay the bills. Duke said that driving a trash truck helped put him through college and he would do it again to help him through this tough patch in business.

Duke drove the trash truck nightly for the greater part of a year, until the economy improved. As a result of his creative thinking and ability to not let his pride get in the way of his success, Duke avoided laying off any employees. Some years later he sold his business for millions of dollars. Duke says that the reason his company was so treasured was greatly due to keeping those employees during the toughest of times. And that if he had not driven that trash truck, he would not have been able to survive during that tough stretch.

When I interviewed Duke, I asked him, "What should people do when they have to take a second job or a position beneath their present standard? What if they are embarrassed to get a job at Walmart or have to drive a trash truck to survive?" His answer was classic Duke Greene, as he simply said, "They should GET OVER IT!" He went on to explain that most people do not look at hardworking people with an eye of pity but think of them as scrappy and determined. People respect you more and will even want to be like you when you work hard! Therefore, do not let your pride poison your prosperity.

1. Here are some lessons from Duke Greene, the "Money Magnet":

2. Making lots of money starts with your thinking. Think about making more money and make it important to make more money.

3. You must discipline yourself and make the commitment to work harder than others think is

necessary. Then it takes routine, repetition, and discipline, especially during tough times.

4. Be willing to hustle, for in time, it will create dividends that allow you to enjoy the fruits of your labor.

5. Make a commitment to be excellent, even in work you don't care for. People who dig for gold or mine for diamonds might not like the initial work, but are willing to do so in order to find true treasures.

6. Make a commitment to strengthen your faith and your mind. Stay close to God, positive materials, and far, far away from negative, small-minded people.

7. If you hang with dummies you will end up being a dummy. Conversely, if you surround yourself with smart people you will end up being brilliant.

8. Get up, get busy, and get selling. You must be willing to sell your ideas, services, and products, or else people will not know you or your product exists. Therefore, if you do not get the word out and market, then you may as well close your business.

9. Study books on entrepreneurism and business, especially the industry you want to be in.

10. Create a plan, even if it is a skimpy plan. For a skimpy plan is better than no plan at all!

11. Read and then re-read *Think & Grow Rich* (which is available here for free at www.williejolley.com/free). That book will help you overcome your doubts and see that others have created wealth out of adversity, and so can you.

12. There are always opportunities around you, but you must be open-minded and visionary to see them. And vision is not about eyesight but about mind-sight!

13. It's better to make money and give it away, than to not make it at all. So make it important to make money!

DR. NIDO QUBEIN, THE WISE WEALTH CREATOR

D r. Nido Qubein came to the United States as a teenager with little knowledge of the American culture and unable to speak the English language. He came with a bag of clothes and $50 in his pocket. His journey since then has been an amazing success story. So much so that the Biography Channel and CNBC have aired his life story, entitled *A Life of Success and Significance.*

Nido Qubein was born in Lebanon, and as a small child his father died leaving his mother to raise five children on her own. She taught young Nido the importance of hard work and education, and when he was 17 years of age she sent him to the United States and gave him some wise advice, "I want you to be great. And to be great, you must walk with the great and talk with the great and learn from them. And always remember to help and serve others along the way!"

Young Nido came to America, got a minor job to make ends meet, and developed a reputation for working hard. He enrolled in Olive College, a small school that he could afford to pay for with his small job. After a couple of years he was able to transfer to the larger High Point University. He did not have enough money for tuition, so he applied for scholarships; because of the reputation he had garnered at Olive College for hard work, an anonymous donor paid his full tuition.

Nido went on to finish his degree at High Point University with honors and then went on to earn his MBA at the University of North Carolina at Greensboro. While still in school he continued to work and saved enough money to buy his first house. Once he purchased his first home, he continued to work hard and bought other real estate in his neighborhood, renting to other students. He continued to scrape and save and buy real estate around town and eventually owned hundreds of properties.

Upon graduation he started his speaking and consulting business, and was so successful that he was able to invest with some others and start a small bank. Over time the bank grew and prospered and was eventually sold to BB&T Bank, due to Nido's hard work, creative thinking, and wisdom. BB&T did not only want to buy the bank but also wanted to have Nido as part of the deal; he was brought on as a director on the BB&T board.

While growing his business and his income, Nido never forgot that his mother told him to walk with the great and always remember to help and serve others. So he joined every chamber and every business group he could and learned from the successful people in those groups. He also remembered how much it meant to him when he was blessed with the tuition payment by the anonymous donor, so he started paying for the tuitions of others who worked hard. Over the years he has given away millions of dollars to students to help with their schooling.

Today, Nido is president of High Point University, an undergraduate and graduate institution with 4,300 students from 40 countries. As a business leader, he is chairman of the Great Harvest Bread Company with 220 stores in 43 states and serves on the boards of several national organizations including BB&T (a Fortune 500 company with $185 billion in assets), the La-Z-Boy Corporation (one of the largest and most recognized furniture brands worldwide), and Dots Stores (a chain of fashion boutiques with more than 400 locations across the country). His board income alone is more than most people earn from their full-time jobs! Yet, that is just a small part of his personal income. He believes that people should always have multiple streams of income so they are not dependent on one income source.

In addition to his business activities, Nido continues to give speeches. As a professional speaker, Nido has received many distinctions, including being awarded the Toastmasters' International Golden Gavel Award and being inducted into the National Speakers' Association Hall of Fame. Additionally, Nido has been the recipient of many honors including the Ellis Island Medal of Honor, along with four U.S. presidents; the Horatio Alger Award for Distinguished Americans, along with Oprah Winfrey; and Citizen of the Year and Philanthropist of the Year in his home city of High Point, North Carolina. He is considered one of the wisest men in business today, and he continues to amaze with his ability to think of wise solutions to difficult problems.

Dr. Nido Qubein shares these wise tips to help you grow your wealth and wisdom:

1. To be all you can be you must have faith and courage. We call this "faithful courage"!

2. Walk with the great people, talk with the great people, and you will become a great person.

3. Who you spend quality time with, is who you will become.

4. A koi fish in a fishbowl will only grow 2 inches, but a koi fish in a lake will grow to a foot. The same is true for you! You will grow proportionally to the environment you are in, so work to be around people and places that allow you to grow to your fullest.

5. Out of adversity can emerge abundance, it is a matter of you seeing the possibilities.

6. Do not shy away from risks, risks bring opportunity. And one cannot be successful without opportunity.

7. Always give without remembering and receive without forgetting.

8. Live one-third of your life earning, live another one-third learning, and live the last third giving and serving.

9. Do not focus on the past. Instead, focus on the future because the past is a wonderful place to visit, but a terrible place to live.

10. Failure can be a great teacher IF you are willing to analyze it. Through analysis of failure you

will learn how and why you failed. And with that knowledge you will gain victory when you try again.

11. You should have God on your side, but more importantly make sure you are on God's side!

12. Use the risk formula to wisely analyze risk. Ask these questions:

    - What is the best that can happen if I take this risk?

    - What is the most likely thing to happen if I take this risk?

    - What is the worst that can happen if I take this risk?

    - Am I willing to live with the worst to get to the best?

13. If the most likely will get you closer to your goal and you are willing to deal with the worst result, then take the risk. Otherwise, walk away!

DAVE STEWARD, THE FAITHFUL FINANCIAL WONDER

Dave Steward is the chairman and founder of America's #1 African American-owned business, World Wide Technology! For almost a decade he has held the #1 money-earner spot on the Black Enterprise Top 100 Money Earners list. Yet, that is not where Dave Steward started. He and his siblings grew up in a small town to hardworking parents who had little money but great faith! Dave earned a basketball scholarship so he could attend college. He worked as hard on his studies as he did on playing basketball, and upon graduation he chose to go to work rather than try to make it in basketball. He felt he was a good basketball player but could be a better businessman. He worked for a number of companies, including FedEx, as a financial analyst.

After working for a few years, Dave decided to start his own business. In the next few years he struggled, but never lost faith. Dave had his car repossessed and almost went bankrupt, yet he refused to give up and continued to trust God.

Due to his hard work and the power of his prayers, he grew the company slowly and surely. Last year, the company reported revenues in excess of $6.5 billion. In addition, *Fortune* magazine ranked his company as "One of the Top 100 Places to Work in America."

Dave was recently inducted into the Horatio Alger Association. He says his faith in God was the secret to his success. In his book *Doing Business by the Good Book,* Dave shares his philosophy for life and business—he was put on this earth to serve others! He sees his company as his pulpit to spread the impact and power of the Word of the Lord.

Dave Steward shares these tips:

1. 1. God expects your best. Know that when you do your very best, you will get blessed.

2. Seek to serve others and good things will always come your way!

3. Count all of life's happenings as joy, even the challenges. It is through the challenges that we grow!

4. It is not easy to build a successful business and successful life, but as steel must go through the fire to become strong, so too must people go through fire to become their best.

5. You must speak things into being. Dave spoke about having a large and thriving company when he was struggling and had no money!

6. Everyone has a measure of faith, but many people will not use their measure of faith. This is a

mistake. Faith must be used and enacted in order to bring maximum results.

7. Do not focus on the present circumstances, but look at the possibilities through the eyes of faith.

8. Our decisions have consequences, so one must learn to make wise decisions.

9. Our brand is the trust level we bring to the marketplace, so we must represent excellence and value to our customers.

10. Put a stake in the ground as to who you will be and what you will stand for. Therefore, take a stand on your values and stay true to them.

CHRIS GARDNER, THE "HAPPYNESS" WEALTH BUILDER

Chris Gardner is an entrepreneur, best-selling author, philanthropist, acclaimed speaker, and, most importantly, a loving parent. Chris is the author of *The Pursuit of Happyness,* an autobiography that became a *New York Times* #1 best-selling book and blockbuster movie starring Will Smith that received Golden Globe, Screen Actors Guild, and Academy Award nominations.

Before his success, Chris Gardner was a hardworking husband and father, who due to adverse circumstances ended up simultaneously homeless and the sole guardian of his toddler son. Unwilling to give up on his son or his dreams, Chris climbed the financial industry ladder from the very bottom. He went from interning to working for Dean Witter Reynolds and Bear Stearns before founding his own brokerage firm and going on to become a multimillionaire.

Chris Gardner, the "Happyness" Wealth Builder, shares these success tips:

1. There is a price to pay for success, and it has nothing to do with money. The price is hard work.

2. Make a commitment to become world class at whatever you do. Not good. Not pretty good. World class!

3. Your future is determined by the decisions you make today, so consistently make wise choices!

4. Wherever you end up, you must take responsibility that you drove there; and if you don't like where you are, you drive to where you want to be!

5. The cavalry is not coming to save you, so you must become your own cavalry!

6. You cannot change something until you own it. Once you own it, set about doing the work to fix it!

7. Commit to your Plan A and work to make it happen. Don't even deal with Plan B because if Plan B were really good, it would be Plan A!

8. To be successful you must be clear-minded, concise in your plan, compelled to make it happen, and consistent in your effort!

9. Surround yourself with people who are positive and who are committed to excellence!

10. Keep learning, keep growing! Learn from life, invest in great books, great people and experiences, and let the world be your classroom!

CAPTAIN CHARLIE PLUMB, THE WEALTHY HERO

Charlie Plumb is a graduate of the United States Naval Academy who went on to become a decorated fighter pilot with 74 successful missions over Vietnam. On his 75th mission, five days before his tour was to end, Charlie was shot down and became a prisoner of war. For six years, Charlie was tortured and held as a POW. When he was finally released, he came home just in time to learn that his wife had divorced him three months earlier and was engaged to marry another man!

Charlie says that he could have chosen to get even, get angry, or get bitter! Instead, he choose to get better and he focused on staying positive. As a result, he didn't get even... he got ahead. Charlie went on to start a business and began speaking about his experiences. He also married a wonderful woman and they have two beautiful children. Charlie now travels the world telling his story of winning through adversity. To date, he has spoken to more than 5,000 audiences and was inducted into the prestigious National Speakers' Association Hall of Fame!

In his inspiring presentation, Charlie tells the story of his survival as a prisoner of war in Vietnam, who was locked in solitary confinement for six years and routinely tortured. He tells how he had to overcome loneliness, fear, pain, and depression and how others can do the same, no matter how difficult their present circumstances. Charlie Plumb uses his story to help others overcome adversity and rise above their limits, whether imposed by others or by themselves. He helps people tap into their inner strength and hope and live life to the fullest.

Here are some tips Captain Charlie Plumb, the Wealthy Hero, shares in his powerful interview:

1. Adversity is a horrible thing to waste! It is through adversity that we grow our success muscle.

2. Within a setback we find the puzzle pieces to our future success!

3. The toughest part of being a prisoner of war was not the physical torture. Instead, it was the doubt and fear that attacks one mentality. Many people are walking around free, but are struggling with those very same fears.

4. You must be willing to look for and find hope, even in situations that look hopeless. There is always a way out! Stay positive and never give up or give in.

5. Whether you think you are a winner or think you are a loser, you are correct! So, keep a winner's

mindset no matter the circumstances, and banish any losing thoughts from your mind.

6. You need faith to help you through those moments when hope is hard to find. With faith, your hope will be rekindled time and time again, leading you out of darkness and into the light of victory.

7. Sometimes we need not pray for God to *move* the mountain. Instead, there are times when we must pray for God to give us the strength to *climb* the mountain.

8. Pray that you find the value within every circumstance. If you can find the value, you will turn short-term pain into long-term growth. Therefore, aim to not just go through challenges, but grow through them!

9. Get rid of a "deserve" mindset, and replace it with an "achievement" mindset. Achievement is where one works, fights for, and creates all that he or she obtains.

10. You must work on your mind and work on your thinking and determine in your own mind that every day is a blessing; and that no matter how bad things get, you still have a chance to turn it around for your good!

Rudy Ruettiger, the Small, Big-Thinking Wealth Builder

RUDY! RUDY! RUDY! That is the chant you hear at the end of the inspirational blockbuster movie, *Rudy*. It is the story of an undersized football player at Notre Dame, who only made the team through sheer grit and determination. After making the team, Rudy stayed on the bench for four straight years. Yet, he inspired his teammates because he never stopped working his hardest or stooped to negative thinking.

In the final game of his career, Rudy was put in the game during the last minute of play and he sacked the opposing team's quarterback to seal his team's win with emphasis. In response, his teammates honored him by carrying Rudy off the field on their shoulders! His story and his YES I CAN attitude has become a source of inspiration for millions of people around the world.

In making the movie *Rudy*, Rudy Ruettiger had to overcome rejection after rejection and setback after setback, but he refused to give up. He kept asking, trying to get funding for the movie, but kept getting doors slammed in his face. Yet he kept asking and kept trying. Eventually someone said YES and his story was told to the world. It has become known as one of the top inspirational movies of all time. In fact, Kobe Bryant shared that the movie *Rudy* was one of the keys to his success as a basketball player! Rudy Ruettiger has become a multimillionaire and a successful businessman.

The following are a few of the great ideas that the small, big-thinking wealth builder Rudy Ruettiger shares in his inspirational interview:

1. The key to success in life is having core values of character, courage, contribution, and commitment.

2. One thought can change your life, for better or for worse, so focus on good thoughts and avoid bad thoughts!

3. You will make mistakes. You will fail. But failing does not make you a failure. On the contrary, failure makes you stronger and smarter. Get up, dust yourself off, and try again until you succeed!

4. Your faith sustains you through tough times! Work daily on developing it so that you have it readily prepared when hard times come your way.

5. Dream big, prepare yourself, and work hard! Dreams make you ready for your moment. Make the most of them!

6. It is okay to be the underdog. Ninety-seven percent of us are underdogs, and if you refuse to give up, the underdog inside you will win!

7. A positive attitude can change your life!

8. If you are not having a great day, change your thinking, and you will change your day!

9. Do what you say you will and be excellent in doing so!

10. Never, ever, ever give up on your dream! If you can dream it, you can do it!

JIM STOVALL,
THE BLIND MILLIONAIRE
MAP MAN

Jim Stovall was an Olympic weightlifting champion and college football star who had expectations of superstardom in sports. As a result of his success as an athlete, he focused only on athletics and not on school. He believed he was destined for a professional football career. During a routine medical examination, he learned he was losing his sight and would be blind in a short time. He had no marketable skills and was flat broke. In fact, he had "negative worth," which meant he was broke and in debt.

On that day, Jim started on a path of self-development and personal growth. He searched to find coaches and mentors who could direct him toward his goal of becoming wealthy. These people made him work on his mind and gave him a detailed course of study that would help him grow. Jim implemented that information and went on to become a multi-millionaire businessman, author, speaker, and philanthropist!

Today, Jim is the author of the worldwide best-selling book *The Ultimate Gift*, which was also made into a popular movie by 20th Century Fox. He has also written a best-selling book telling his personal life lessons for wealth building entitled *The Millionaire Map.* In addition to writing and speaking, Jim has produced other movies and runs an Emmy Award-winning television network that caters to blind viewers. In the year 2000, Jim was selected as the International Humanitarian of the Year, joining Jimmy Carter and Mother Teresa.

Here are ten success tips Jim Stovall, the Blind Millionaire Map Man, shares in his uplifting interview:

1. Life is not about what happens to you, but what you do about it!

2. Money must be seen as a tool that allows you to do what you love. Money gives you options and allows you to live on your own terms.

3. Money magnifies everything. "If you love doing good, then money allows you to do more good. But if you love doing stupid stuff, it will allow you to do more of that as well." So make money and do good with the money you make.

4. Never buy a map from someone who has never been where you want to go. Instead, be willing to ask for help from those who have been where you want to go.

5. The quickest way to get to wealth is to make up your mind to do whatever it takes, that is

moral and legal, to achieve it! Then go to work on that goal.

6. Starting is half the battle of success! Remember, a good plan poorly executed is better than a perfect plan that is never executed.

7. Change your mind and you can change your life. You have the right to choose your path. You are one quality decision away from anything you want.

8. Do not let small challenges become big obstacles. Having no sight is tough, but having no vision is tragic! Sight is used to see where you are, but vision is used to see where you will go and who you will become.

9. You cannot expand your bank account until you expand your mind. Therefore, invest in exposing your mind to informative and uplifting content within self-improvement books, audio lessons, videos, and live seminars.

10. Take note of this fact: poor people have big TVs and very small personal libraries; whereas, billionaires have big TVs as well, but HUGE personal libraries!

FINAL THOUGHTS BY DR. WILLIE JOLLEY

I am so glad you are reading this last part of the book because that probably signifies that you have read the whole book. I think back to when I started reading books and how I often struggled to finish them. I would pick up a book and then put it down and never finish it; but one day I read a book from start to finish and I felt a rush come over me. I not only felt a sense of accomplishment, but also learned that there were pearls that came at the end of the book that I would have missed if I had not finished it.

Most importantly, I learned that the Willie Jolley who finished the book was not the same Willie Jolley who had picked up the book initially. I had grown and stretched and become a different person. I have since described the Willie Jolley who had finished the book as a person who had a successful "brain transplant"! I took the information that came out of the brain of the author and transplanted it into my brain, and therefore I was a new and improved person.

I am glad you are at the end of this book, and I pray that the content and these interviews have inspired you to think bigger and bolder. I pray that you will now do something magnificent with the information you have absorbed through these pages. *Dream big* and then *do big!* Make a commitment to take your setback and turn the experience into a stellar comeback, and then turn that comeback into money—greenbacks!

Finally, I pray that you will share this book and the inspiration you have received from it with others who can also grow and stretch because of the information. I have learned that when you help someone else, you help yourself, because what you give is what you get! And you cannot put perfume on someone else without getting a little on yourself. So share this book and the interviews and watch them grow as you have grown.

I close this book with the thought that a gentleman told me on a plane when I was at one of my low points, "Keep the faith! And remember your best is yet to come!" I send you forward with that thought and that blessing on your life! Your best truly is yet to come! So...go live your dreams!

And remember, your setbacks are nothing but setups for amazing comebacks—then turn those comebacks into massive greenbacks!

And always help others as you help yourself!

God bless you!

ABOUT THE AUTHOR

DR. WILLIE JOLLEY is truly a renaissance man! He is an award-winning speaker and singer, a best-selling author, and a popular radio and television personality. He is the CEO of Willie Jolley Worldwide, a professional development organization that focuses on developing excellence in corporate and individual performance. He is also the chairman of the board of the non-profit ministry organization, Jolley Good News.

In 1999, Dr. Jolley was named One of the Outstanding Five Speakers in the World by Toastmasters International, and in 2005, he was inducted into the Speakers Hall of Fame. He is a five-time Washington area (WAMMIE) award-winning singer. His television broadcasts are seen on PBS and CBS Television, and his radio broadcasts are heard weekends on SiriusXM Radio and daily on numerous stations across the country.

Dr. Jolley is the author of several international best-selling books including *It Only Takes a Minute to Change Your Life* and *A Setback Is a Setup for a Comeback, Turn Setbacks into Greenbacks, and An Attitude of Excellence,* which was endorsed by Dr. Stephen Covey. His new "Willie Jolley" music is now the number one downloaded motivational music on the Apple iTunes site.

Dr. Jolley regularly speaks for top corporations and organizations around the world. His clients include Walmart, Dell, Ford, Verizon, Marriott, DuPont, Nabisco, Chevron, Dominos, Amway, Prudential, McDonald's, Chase Manhattan, Allstate Insurance, Pepsi, Coca-Cola, Sprint, Borders Books, Prudential of Australia, American Society of Association Executives, and the U.S. Army, Navy, and Marines. In addition, his program for youth, Dare 2 Dream, is one of the top-selling youth videos in the United States.

Dr. Jolley holds a Doctorate of Ministry in Faith-Driven Achievement from the California Graduate School of Theology, a Master's in Theology from Wesley Theological seminary, and a Bachelor's in Psychology and Sociology from American University. His mission in life is to help people maximize their God-given talents and abilities so they can do more, be more, and achieve more! He and his family live in Washington, DC.

DR. WILLIE JOLLEY
SUCCESS PRODUCTS

Business Building Products

- Jolley Virtual Transformation (Digital Interactive Training & Development)
- JolleyVT.Com
- An Attitude of Excellence Book & CD
- Double Your Business (Live in Australia) DVD
- The Will To Win Seminar DVD
- T.I.P.S. for Speaking Success: DVDs & CDs
  - The Entrepreneur's Rich Success Treasure Chest: DVDs & CDs
  - Turn Setbacks Into Comebacks PBS Special on DVD
  - Dr. Willie Jolley SiriusXM Radio Wealthy Ways Show Interviews

Motivational/Inspirational Products

- An Attitude of Excellence book
- Money Making Music & Motivation: DVD & CDs
  - A Setback Is A Setup for a Comeback!: Book, CDs or DVD
  - It Only Takes a Minute to Change Your Life: Book or CDs
  - The Willie Jolley Jazz/Gospel Combo: CDs
- Youth Motivational Deluxe Package: PBS DVD & Parent and Student Guides
- Chicken Soup for the Christian Soul, II: Book & CD
- The Will To Win – Seminar on DVD

Preview or Purchase these Products & More at: